RUGBY LE▮

in the 'Sixties

VOLUME TWO

For fans who don't want to forget

RUGBY LEAGUE JOURNAL
PUBLISHING

Volume Two in the 'Rugby League Journal History Series'

This book is dedicated to every boy's hero of the 'sixties

First published in Great Britain in 2011 by
Rugby League Journal Publishing
P.O.Box 22, Egremont, Cumbria, CA23 3WA

ISBN 978-09548355-6-9

Written, edited and designed by Harry Edgar
ICT production consultant: Ruth Edgar
Printed by Printexpress (Cumbria) Limited

Front cover pictures: Vince Karalius, Ian Brooke and Billy Boston.
Frontispiece picture: Vince Karalius in the Swinton Ashes Test match of November 1963.
Dedication picture: Les Lowther watched over by Blackpool Tower.

RUGBY LEAGUE JOURNAL

PUBLISHING

P.O. Box 22, Egremont, Cumbria, CA23 3WA
E-Mail: rugbyleague.journal@virgin.net   Telephone: 01946 817270
www.rugbyleaguejournal.net

Contents

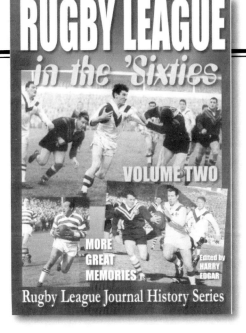

"How do, Dennis," ... "Aw reet, Harold,"
The 'sixties may be remembered as an innocent
time when Prime Ministers and prop-forwards
could get together without worrying about
security passes, and chat about anything from feet
up in the scrums to joining the Common Market.
But you could always bet that some Rugby League
club official somewhere was complaining about
something - television, the rules, the fixtures ...

Special thanks to Eddie Whitham

*Most of the colour pictures in this book which provide a
rare and vivid insight to Rugby League in the 1960s are
from the camera of Eddie Whitham. We are grateful to
Eddie for his contribution which includes the never before
seen pictures of the 1967 Kangaroo touring team's games
at Warrington, St.Helens and Widnes.*

*Our thanks also to all the photographers whose skills
have provided so many fine images - with so many old
pictures from private collections it is often difficult to
ascertain their origins, thus there has been no intention to
breach anybody's copyright.*

*You can order further copies of this book by sending
a cheque for £14.95 (including postage & packing)
per copy - payable to 'Rugby League Journal' to:
Rugby League Journal,
P. O. Box 22,
Egremont,
Cumbria,
CA23 3WA.*

*You can also order our quarterly magazine
"Rugby League Journal"
price £3.95 for a single issue or £15 for annual
subscription (4 issues).
Also available on-line from our website:
www.rugbyleaguejournal.net*

At the heart of the 'Sixties in British Rugby League, Peter Smethurst and Bob Irving - two of the outstanding players of the decade - in action for Oldham in a match against Leigh. We won't forget.

Introduction

When we produced our first volume looking back on Rugby League in the 'sixties we promised there would be a follow up, and here it is. More nostalgia, and more fascinating snapshots into what is now the dim and distant history of the game but, which to many of us, seems just like yesterday. The main aim of this book is to entertain by allowing readers to go back, in many cases to their own childhoods, and be reminded of the players, teams and events they grew up with. But, as always with anything vaguely historical, we would love to be able to fire up the imaginations of the younger generation by helping them learn something new about the heritage of Rugby League.

As a schoolboy in the 'sixties myself, and already an avid Rugby League fan, I was fascinated to learn about its history and the great men and their deeds of long ago. In my case, it was being told about pre-War heroes like Jim Brough, Martin Hodgson and Jim Sullivan, then the immaculate Gus Risman. And there was always a great fascination with the men off the field who promoted the game and led it on so many new adventures, most especially Lance Todd, John Wilson and Harry Sunderland. I was lucky to go to a Junior school whose headmaster, Mr. Lance Fitzsimmons, was a dedicated Rugby League man, who took great pride in the game's local roots in its coal-mining communities, and who instilled into his pupils the same sense of fair play, discipline and respect for authority that he always expected to see on the Rugby League field.

Mr. Fitzsimmons taught us about history by showing us an old Cumberland cap won by his uncle Kit, who played full-back for the county in the earliest Northern Union days; and I can remember clearly one day in assembly in 1964 when our headmaster broke off from prayers and announcements to inform the school that a great man had passed away - Harry Sunderland. Soon after, Mr. Fitzsimmons was organising something he said had long been his ambition, a trip to the Rugby League Cup Final at Wembley for his pupils. He had been waiting to get the right group whom he knew were so keen on the game they would really appreciate going to Wembley and have their enthusiasm boosted even more. It certainly had the desired effect in my case as we headed down to London to see Widnes play Hull Kingston Rovers.

Jim Brough and Jeff Bawden - Rugby League mentors in the 'sixties.

Our first volume on the 'sixties published last year proved to be extremely popular, and I was delighted that it appeared to bring so much pleasure to so many people - which is, basically, the number one aim of our quarterly magazine *"Rugby League Journal,"* now approaching its tenth year. Of course, with this Volume Two we want to present totally new material, so we have to take a slightly different approach. In Volume One we presented all the facts and figures of so many aspects of the game in the 'sixties, including all the major Finals and statistics of all the international games. In this Volume Two we go more off the beaten track in remembering wider various aspects of the game, with a much more personal approach. We have also included a scrapbook page on each and every one of the thirty professional clubs that made up the game in England in the eventful decade that was the 'sixties, so fans from all those clubs can enjoy their own local memories.

I have to admit, I love the nostalgia of the 'sixties because I loved the way Rugby League was back then - with the international matches and tours such a vibrant part of the game and every club in the League feeling they were part of something big, able to approach the start of every Challenge Cup campaign with a genuine hope that this could be their Wembley year. I will always be grateful to my mentors of the 'sixties who taught me about the game, fine men like Jim Brough, Jeff Bawden and Ron Morgan. And it is my pleasure to try and pass on some of that knowledge I have gleaned over the years for our readers to enjoy. This is the second book in our "Rugby League Journal History Series" - my hope is that there will be many more on various areas of the game and its heritage which I hold dear.

HARRY EDGAR (Editor "Rugby League Journal")

RIDERS ON A STORM

(Above)
The greatest South African signing of them all - Tom Van Vollenhoven - doing his best to evade the Swinton defence before a packed crowd at Knowsley Road in 1961-62. John Stopford is the Swinton man on the right.

(Above)
Always the fans' favourite - Billy Boston signs an autograph during the 1962 Lions tour.

Rugby League rode a storm throughout the 1960s as it battled against huge social changes which made it more and more challenging for the game to maintain the attendance levels it had enjoyed in the previous decade. Television was becoming a significant factor and, whilst the working people of the north of England may have had more money in their pockets than ever before, they also had many more things to spend it on.

That challenge certainly kept the game's administrators on their toes and nobody could ever accuse Rugby League in the 'sixties of being afraid to try something new. The game led the way for British sport in pioneering the use of substitutes (in 1964) and then Sunday matches (in 1967); it accepted live Saturday afternoon television coverage on the BBC and Sunday lunchtime coverage of amateur games on commercial television; it took the first steps into branded sponsorships; and it backed its clubs who invested in floodlights. Those lights helped the BBC launch their new second channel when the revolutionary Floodlit Trophy began to be broadcast on Tuesday nights and became the Corporation's "guinea pig" for producing live sports coverage on BBC 2.

Despite the restricted communications of the day, Rugby League did its best to help the game's expansion overseas in the early part of the decade. As the 'sixties dawned, the Australians played two matches in Italy at the end of their Kangaroo tour, whilst the French played an amateur international in Yugoslavia, and then great efforts were made to help the development of the game in South Africa. Both the Great Britain touring team and the Wakefield Trinity club played matches in South Africa in 1962, before the first "Springbok" Rugby League tour to Australia and New Zealand took place in 1963. South Africa had become a prolific source of player recruitment for the English clubs (which, no doubt, did much to fuel the Rugby Union's resentment of the League code in that country) - the vast majority of signings proved to be failures, but there were a handful of gems including: Tom Van Vollenhoven and Len Killeen (St.Helens), Fred Griffiths (Wigan), Alan Skene and Gert Coetzer (Wakefield), Wilf Rosenberg (Leeds) and Piet Pretorious (Workington), who helped light up many winter Saturday afternoons in the north of England.

International competition still remained as the very heartbeat of Rugby League in the 'sixties, with all four major nations maintaining the regular schedule of tours. Great Britain's two Lions tours, in 1962 and 1966, yielded substantial profits for the British game and, whilst the Ashes were won so spectacularly by Eric Ashton's team in 1962, the Test team of 1966, captained by Brian Edgar, were desperately unlucky not to do likewise. Meanwhile France, after maintaining their record of never losing a Test series in Australia on their 1960 tour, found the going much tougher in 1964 and finally succumbed to the green and golds.

As for the Kangaroo tours, history was made in 1963 when an all-Australian team won the Ashes on British soil for the first time; and they were retained four years later in 1967. The world Rugby League inhabited in England had changed significantly in the four years between those Kangaroo tours, as constant bickering over falling crowds created an air of desperation among many club officials. But still the ruling body, under the guidance of its secretary Bill Fallowfield, remained staunchly internationalist. Again leading the way for other sports, two World Cup tournaments were held in the 'sixties, the third in 1960 and the fourth in 1968. The initial plan for the 1960 tournament in England had been to stage matches under floodlights at big soccer grounds, but that idea was scuppered by the Football League. The Rugby League had better luck when again it broke new ground by staging an Ashes Test in both the 1963 and 1967 series under floodlights at London venues.

The game's search for solutions to its problems led to non-stop arguments about both the fixture format and the rules of the game on the field, with Bill Fallowfield a prolific writer on both subjects in the League's numerous official programmes for big games, and in newspapers. The league was split into two divisions in 1962-63, but the new format was scrapped only two years into a three-year trial period. With the one league system restored in 1964-65, with it came a top-16 play-off to decide the Champions rather than the tried and trusted top-four of previous years. The most dramatic change to the game on the field came in 1966 with the introduction of the four-tackle rule - much to the delight of its architect Fallowfield who, for many years, had campaigned for changes to be made to stop one team hogging possession.

The 'sixties was the decade when, thanks largely to television, new horizons began to open up for young people from the towns of the north of England where Rugby League played such a major part in their communities. But still most of the game's players worked in the north's traditional industries of the mines and the mills, on the docks in Hull or at the Shipyards in Barrow. Despite all its soul-searching in the corridors of power, to the fans out on the terraces, Rugby League was a huge amount of fun in the 1960s. Challenge Cup ties managed to draw some remarkable crowds, with the numerous midweek afternoon replays adding to the drama; the international game created so much focus for players and supporters as well as much media attention; and there was the ever-present adverts for Jim Windsor's fixed odds coupons for the adults which led to much entertainment for the youngsters with Jim's action-packed "Annuals."

(Above)
Bill Fallowfield sits on the touchline bench with Great Britain's non-playing reserves, Dick Huddart and Bill Thompson of Widnes, at a Test match in France in 1962. It would still be another couple of years before substitutes were allowed. Despite his critics, Fallowfield always maintained a good relationship with the players.

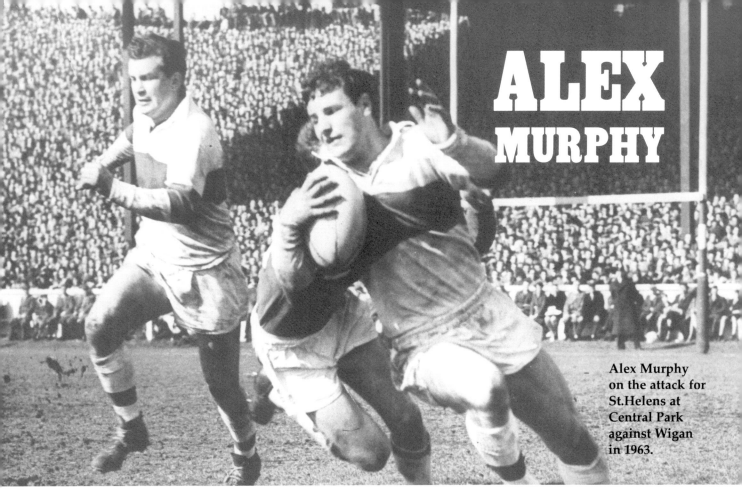

ALEX MURPHY

Alex Murphy on the attack for St.Helens at Central Park against Wigan in 1963.

The '60s most sensational star

(Above)
Alex Murphy playing for Great Britain on tour in Australia. Alex's brilliance lit up the Sydney Cricket Ground in 1962 as Great Britain stormed in to retain the Ashes.

Rugby League saw many brilliant stars shine during the 1960s, plenty - like Neil Fox, Dick Huddart, Alan Hardisty or Tommy Bishop - made a huge impact throughout the decade both at home and abroad. But no individual was more sensational than Alex Murphy. As a teenager, Alex had already shown his brilliance in 1958 on tour in Australia and in 1959 at home in St.Helens' Championship winning team - but once the 'sixties arrived, Murphy ruled the roost.

Sensation and controversy seemed to go hand in glove with Alex as he became the game's highest profile personality, never shy of giving the media plenty to write about. But he started the decade concentrating on doing what he did best - playing brilliant Rugby League - as he achieved the pinnacle of success in the space of three fantastic years. In 1960 he was a World Cup winner; in 1961 he revelled at Wembley as St.Helens beat Wigan in the Challenge Cup Final; and in 1962 he hit his abolute peak on the hard grounds of Australia as a star of the Great Britain team which won the Ashes and went within a controversial whisker of becoming the first British side to win a cleansweep of all three Tests.

There was nothing Alex couldn't do, they called him cocky, a big mouth, you name it ... he took it, and always had the last laugh by producing the match-winning goods on the field. But, whilst captaining Saints to one of the most successful seasons in their history, 1965-66, in which they went close to achieving the magical feat of winning "All Four Cups," the first signs of trouble began to appear that would ultimately lead to the biggest controversy of his career. Despite all the success, which included a Cup and Championship "double," Alex was unhappy at having to play in the centre. He had been moved out to the threequarters to accomodate Saints' new signing Tommy Bishop at number seven. Bishop was picked as Great Britain's first choice scrum-half for the 1966 tour, whilst Murphy turned down the opportunity to make his third Lions tour, disappointed at being overlooked for the captaincy.

Alex informed the St.Helens club that he would no longer play out of position at centre, and the dispute escalated to the point where he was refused training facilities at Knowsley Road. Eventually, on 26th September 1966, Murphy put in a written transfer request to the Saints chairman. "I felt I might as well be playing elsewhere as hanging about at St.Helens," said Alex about that controversial time which led to him leaving his home town club. The transfer request was granted, but the fee of £12,000 asked by Saints was, according to Murphy: "unrealistic and ridiculous." That's when it became public that the Australian club North Sydney had offered him a lucrative four year contract to go and play down-under, a move that would also have brought St.Helens an £8,000 transfer fee for his release. Alex was on the verge of signing the contract and emigrating to Australia, when his story took another dramatic twist - one that would take him not to far away Sydney, but just a few miles down the East Lancs. Road to Leigh.

Murphy shocked the Rugby League world by accepting a five year deal, in which he was to be paid £30-a-week, to become the coach of Leigh. It was one of the most controversial moments in Alex's sensational career. St.Helens were stunned because they couldn't recoup a penny in transfer fees as Murphy was going just as a coach, not a player. They quickly received a £5,000 bid from Wigan for his services (*see below*) but, eventually, Leigh chairman Major Jack Rubin managed to sort out a deal with Saints for Murphy's transfer as a player to Hilton Park ... and another eventful and colourful chapter in Alex's sensational story was about to be written.

(Above) **Aircraftman A. J. Murphy pictured at the dart-board during his National Service days in the early 'sixties. Alex's first biography, published in 1967, was titled** *"Saints Hit Double Top."* **Whilst in the Royal Air Force, Murphy starred in Services Rugby Union matches.**

When Wigan bid 5,000 for Alex

This letter *(right)* was from the Wigan club secretary Ken Senior, addressed to his counterpart at St.Helens, Mr. Basil Lowe, and dated 14th October 1966. It reads:
"Dear Basil,
Further to our telephone conversation this morning, I wish to confirm our offer of £5,000 for the transfer of Alex. Murphy to Wigan.
Yours sincerely,
K. Senior
Secretary.

WIGAN FOOTBALL CLUB LTD.
AFFILIATED WITH THE RUGBY FOOTBALL LEAGUE

TELEPHONE: Ground – WIGAN 43079

REGISTERED OFFICE:
CENTRAL PARK
WIGAN

DIRECTORS:—
Chairman: Mr. H. S. WEBSTER
Vice-Chairman: Mr. L. K. BROOME
Mr. W. Ackers
Mr. S. Baxendale
Mr. N. Bibby
Mr. H. T. Gostelow
Mr. J. Hilton
Mr. E. Roper
Mr. M. Ryan
Mr. W. Wood
Secretary: Mr. K. SENIOR

Mr. B. Lowe,
Secretary,
St. Helens Football Club Ltd.,
Knowsley Road,
ST. HELENS.

14th October, 1966.

Dear Basil,

Further to our telephone conversation this morning, I wish to confirm our offer of £5,000 for the transfer of Alex. Murphy to Wigan.

Yours sincerely,

K. Senior

Secretary.

Wembley winners in 1963 - Coetzer, Turner, Brooke, Pearman, Greenwood and Neil Fox.

Glory days in the Merrie City

(Above)
Skipper Derek Turner with Harold Poynton and Jack Wilkinson at Wembley in 1963 - key men in Trinity's Wembley glory years.

(Right)
Rocky's team - Wakefield Trinity in 1961-6. Left to right: *(Standing):* **Gerry Round, Jan Prinsloo, Dennis Williamson, Geoff Oakes, Jack Wilkinson, Brian Briggs, Milan Kosanovic, Don Vines.** *(Seated):* **Fred Smith, Alan Skene, Ken Rollin, Derek Turner (captain), Keith Holliday, Albert Firth and Neil Fox.**

They call Wakefield the Merrie City ... it'll certainly be merry tonight ... were the words conjured up by BBC television commentator Eddie Waring as he watched Wakefield Trinity run round Wembley with the Challenge Cup on their lap of honour in 1962. And Eddie was right.

Wakefield was the "in" place to be for Rugby League in the early 'sixties as Trinity enjoyed the glamour of making three trips to Wembley in the first four years of the decade. The city, and its Rugby League team, was the setting for the highly acclaimed film *"This Sporting Life,"* starring Richard Harris with one of the dodgiest attempts at a Yorkshire accent you'll ever hear. That it should be based on Wakefield was fitting as the author of the book that led to the film was David Storey, a native of the city, and it was released in 1963 as part of the vogue of movies described by the critics as "gritty northern social realism."

If films like that portrayed life as "grim up north," the reality was that Wakefield was a very vibrant and happy city thanks almost entirely to the entertainment and good times provided its Rugby League club. Trinity had won three Challenge Cups by 1963, and then - with a largely different team in what seemed an entirely different world - finally got their hands on the Championship in 1967, retaining it in 1968 a week before losing so cruelly at Wembley in the infamous "Watersplash Final." Constant factors throughout the decade, who participated in both the early and later successes, were stand-off

Harold Poynton and the points machine Neil Fox. Both were Lance Todd Trophy winners in the 1962 and '63 Wembley triumphs, and both were among the five Trinity players (the others were Derek Turner, Gerry Round and Jack Wilkinson) who toured to Australia with the successful 1962 Lions. And Poynton was the man who took over the captaincy when "Rocky" Turner retired and skippered Wakefield to their two Championships in 1967 and '68.

Trinity's popularity and the pride they engendered in their home city owed much to the fact that, despite being a galaxy of stars of their time, they were largely a team of local boys. In the first of the Wembley finals in 1960, of the handful who weren't born and bred in or close to Wakefield, they were still all Yorkshire lads who hailed from "faraway" places like: Batley (John Etty), Hebden Bridge (Gerry Round) or Halifax (Jack Wilkinson.) Winger Fred Smith had been born in Manchester but raised in Yorkshire, and the only real "outsider" was South African centre Alan Skene.

In the years that followed, South Africans continued to be Wakefield's main source of imports, with Colin Greenwood and Gert "Oupa" Coetzer following in Skene's footsteps. The only other non locals were the occasional Cumbrian - Dennis Williamson in 1962 and Matt McLeod in 1968 - Welshman Don Vines and a Yugoslavian hooker who learned his Rugby League in Halifax, Milan Kosanovic. Another Cumbrian, scrum-half Joe Bonnar, featured in the 1968 team and his name was actually listed in Wembley programme, but he missed the "Watersplash Final" and was replaced by a Lancastrian, Ray Owen from Widnes. That local pride and sense of community surrounding the team in Wakefield was illustrated by the sight of regular adverts in the Trinity official programme for businesses including: Derek Turner's Removals in Ossett, Harold Poynton's Newsagents shop; Ian Brooke's Gas and Central Heating; Neil Fox's Turf Accountants; or Ken Hirst's pub the Tawny Owl Inn at Ossett. The Merrie City clearly owed much to the men of Wakefield Trinity.

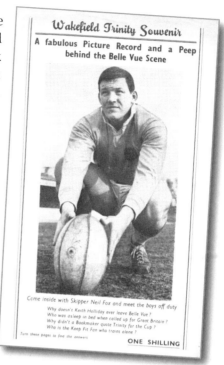

(Above) **A popular souvenir for Trinity fans.** *(Below)* **Richard Harris in** *"This Sporting Life."*

The 'sixties style in Wakefield

Keeping up with fashions in the early 'sixties - these three lovely young ladies were the Geary sisters: Peggy, Molly and Lily, who all grew up in Lupset, Wakefield. All three married well known Wakefield Trinity players: Albert "Budgie" Firth, Stanley Smith and Les Chamberlain, respectively. As was usual in those days, all three were local lads, Albert Firth coming from Stanley - three miles away from Trinity's Belle Vue ground, Stanley Smith from Agbrigg - all of 200 yards away, and Les Chamberlain from Middleton - a huge nine miles away. In 1960, Bramley made a double swoop and signed both Smith and Chamberlain, and this photograph of the three sisters, with best hair-dos in place, was taken at the Barley Mow in 1961 as they watched their menfolk do battle. Bramley were playing Trinity, the latter with Albert Firth in their team and playing against two of his brothers-in-law.

Dedicated followers of fashion

(Above)
Big was beautiful as Bradford Northern became the game's most fashionable team in the mid-'sixties, less than 12 months after the club was reborn in 1964. This picture was taken in September 1965, by which time Northern had built a mighty forward pack comprising of, *left to right:* **Gil Ashton (5ft. 11 in., 14st. 4lb.), Alan Hepworth (5ft. 11 in., 14st. 2lb.), Terry Ackerley (5ft. 11in, 13st. 8lb.), Jack Hirst (6ft. 1in. 16st. 8lb.), Johnny Rae (6ft. 2in., 14st. 5lb), and Terry Clawson (6ft, 15st. 10lb.)**

The look of Rugby League began to change in the 1960s, although all teams could still be relied upon to wear polished black boots with white laces. Clean cut was the order of the day in a Rugby League world seemingly untouched by the popular fashions of the Beatles and the beat music craze, or later the hippie look (long flowing locks and facial hair were destined to arrive in the game in the following decade of the 'seventies).

The 'sixties saw a new awareness among several clubs to create something "bright and modern" in the way their teams turned out, and leading the way were Swinton - the club so quintissentially linked with the "Swinging Sixties." After wearing plain blue jerseys previously throughout their history, Swinton emerged in the 'sixties with the radical new look of a bold white vee on their chests, accompanied by the badge of a rampant lion. They were the first team to wear all white socks which always looked "whiter than white," as the Lions never failed to appear in pristine outfits, with white starched collars on their royal blue jerseys turned up. This was the look of class so familar at Station Road and throughout the game in 1963 and 1964 as Swinton won the Championship in the two consecutive seasons of Rugby League's experiment with two divisions.

As Swinton's star began to fade somewhat in the second half of the 'sixties it was Bradford Northern who emerged as Rugby League's trendsetters. After the nadir of them dropping out of the league in 1964, the new Northern came back on a wave of new optimism promoted by their charismatic directors Joe Phillips and Trevor Foster (both former players at Odsal Stadium.) The crowds came flocking back to Odsal as Bradford became one of the best supported

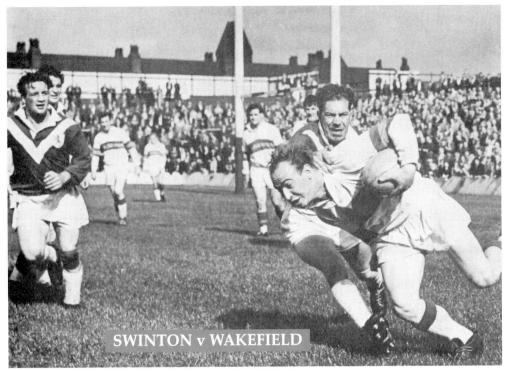

SWINTON v WAKEFIELD

(Left)
Swinton's classic look of the Championship winning seasons of 1962-63 and 1963-64, pictured as they took on the equally distinctively attired Wakefield Trinity at Station Road. The picture shows Swinton's captain Albert Blan tackling Trinity's South African winger Jan Prinsloo

clubs in Rugby League, famed for taking a large following of thousands to away games, all colourfully dressed in their red, amber and black colours. Northern were pioneers in introducing cheer girls, dressed as majorettes, and their team's appearance on the field was immediately amended to distinguish them from the "old" (and, latterly, so unsuccessful) Bradford Northern. The "new" Northern were kitted out in almost all white, a pristine look with the white sleeves which gave the impression of the familar red, amber and black band being stretched out across the barrel chests of their giants forwards. In reality, Bradford's forwards were probably no bigger than many other club's forwards, but that white kit made them appear like giants as they took the long walk down the Odsal steps ready to do battle on the turf below.

Bradford also introduced a unique fashion trend in the late 'sixties by wearing numbers on the front of their jerseys - something no other club in English Rugby League did. It was something almost exclusively associated with the game in Queensland - why Bradford Northern became the only English club to have numbers on their fronts was a mystery, but it is likely that their post-1964 influx of Queenslanders like Garth Budge was the source of the idea.

Hunslet were another club who made a distinctive fashion choice when they decided to rekindle their original colours of chocolate and white in 1962. After becoming synonymous with the famous myrtle, white and flame colours, the Parksiders introduced a very carefully designed alternative chocolate and white outfit in 1962-63 season, which featured two chocolate hoops, navy blue shorts and a very deliberate thick and thin hoops on the socks. Hunslet also broke the Rugby League fashion mould for a while with this kit by abandoning collars and having a crew neck style jersey. Later, Hunslet were to adapt their "chocolate" kit to white with a vee, which is the outfit they wore with such distinction at Wembley in 1965.

Castleford, as a team which blossomed in the 'sixties to revel in the tag of "Classy Cas," did so with a style which looked so modern - saying goodbye to their traditional hoops to wear the bright all yellow jerseys with black collars. Meanwhile St.Helens first wore the "red vee" that was to become their trademark in the 1961 Challenge Cup Final versus Wigan. It was to be the 1965-66 season before Saints switched permanently to the "red vee."

(Above)
Brian Gabbitas, the Hunslet stand-off, in the distinctively designed chocolate and white outfits, with crew necks and no collars, introduced by the Parksiders in 1962-63.

Beating the transfer ban

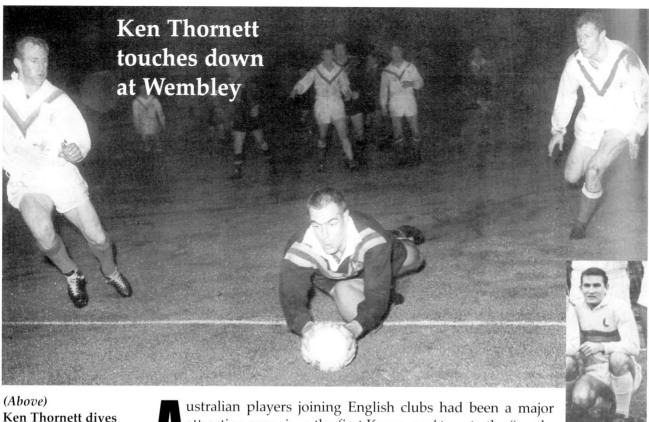

Ken Thornett touches down at Wembley

Australian players joining English clubs had been a major attraction ever since the first Kangaroos' tour to the "mother land" in 1908, but throughout the 1950s the transfer ban had stopped the recruitment of stars from Aussie Rugby League. The aim of the ban was to help rebuild the strength of the Australian Test team by halting the talent drain to England which had gone into overdrive in the years immediately after World War Two. In the meantime, those English clubs still eager to boost their ranks with the "glamour" of an Aussie or two, turned to Australian Rugby Union players with no little success.

The ban continued into the 'sixties, with only a handful of Rugby League players being given clearance to spend time with English clubs, either on short term "guest" arrangements or "working holidays" by amateur players. Some players from Queensland did manage to get round the problems of getting a clearance, notably the State representative threequarter Lionel Williamson who joined Halifax in the 1964-65 season. He was to enjoy greater success when he left Thrum Hall and moved to Odsal later in 1965, scoring 25 tries in 48 games for Bradford Northern. Williamson returned to Australia to become an international winger, starring in the Aussies' winning World Cup Finals of 1968 and 1970. Bradford signed another couple of young Queenslanders in 1964-65, Errol Stock and Garth Budge - the latter stayed in England to become a key figure in the Rugby League's National Coaching Scheme. But, by far the most successful Aussie in England in the early 'sixties was full-back Ken Thornett, a star of the Leeds 1961 Championship team.

COLOUR OF THE 'SIXTIES

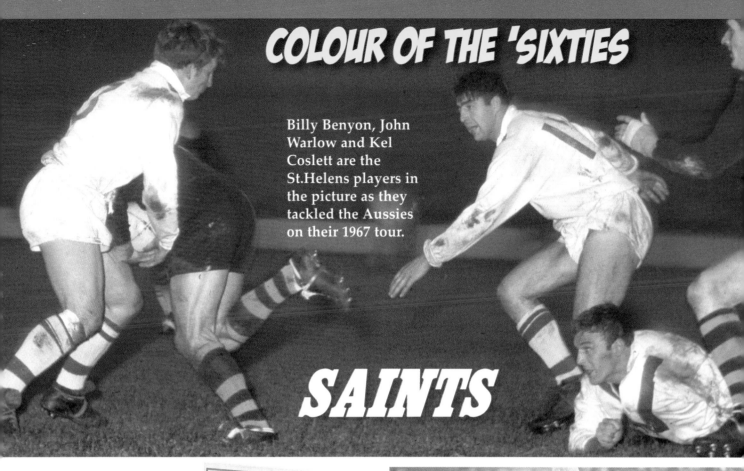

Billy Benyon, John Warlow and Kel Coslett are the St.Helens players in the picture as they tackled the Aussies on their 1967 tour.

SAINTS

IVOR LINGARD
PARRAMATTA EELS

FIVE EIGHTH

In the 'sixties, British Rugby League players who went to Australia enjoyed a California-type life-style very different to the north of England. It's a safe bet that Ivor Lingard was the first lad from Featherstone ever to have his face on his very own bubblegum card.

BRADFORD NORTHERN

Tommy Smales and Johnny Rae force an opponent into touch for Bradford Northern in 1965-66.

LEEDS

Barry Seabourne guides the Leeds attack at Headingley.

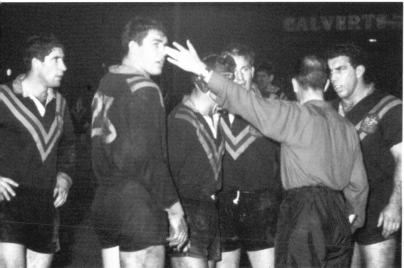

(Pictured) Illustrations of how the Australians found it tough going against English club sides on the 1967 Kangaroo tour as three floodlit matches against Wigan, St.Helens and Widnes all saw their players in the wars under the close eye of the referees.

(Above)
Reg Gasnier wrapped up against the cold on the 1963 Kangaroo tour, returned in 1967 as captain-coach as Australia retained the Ashes but lost the Test series in France.

Gasnier was one of the game's greatest stars in the 'sixties after shooting to prominence on the 1959-60 Kangaroo tour. He returned to England for the 1960 World Cup and then for the '63 and '67 Kangaroo tours.

The 1963-64 Australian touring team to Europe. Left to right: *(Back row):* J.Raper, P.Gallagher, G.Wilson, G.Langlands, K.Ryan, P.Quinn, K.Smyth, B.Hambly. *(Third row):* J.Cleary, K.Thornett, R.Gasnier, P.Dimond, J.Lisle, M.Cleary, K.Day, R.Thornett. *(Second row):* K.Irvine, Mr.A.Sparks (manager), A.Summons (Captain), I.Walsh (Vice-captain), Mr.J.Lynch (Manager), N.Kelly, *(Front row):* E.Harrison, L.Johns, F.Stanton, B. Muir and B.Rushworth. (Absent: J. Gleeson).

To become a Kangaroo by going away on a tour to England and France was the greatest ambition of every Australian Rugby League player, and the visit of the men in the classic green and gold outfits was a special highlight eagerly awaited every four years by the game in Europe.

The 1963 Kangaroos shook British Rugby League to its foundations by becoming the first all Australian team to win the Ashes on English soil, and they did it spectacularly with a 50-12 thrashing of Great Britain in the "massacre" of Station Road, Swinton in the second Test. On that November day in the suburbs of Manchester, both teams stood for a minute's silent tribute to the assassinated American President John F. Kennedy. The Australians injured captain-coach Arthur Summons had to watch from the sidelines as his team won the Ashes, but his inspirational speeches in the dressing-rooms were a key factor in the Aussies' success.

In total, the 1963 tourists played 22 fixtures in England, before going on to play another 14 in France (with a 15th at Lyon being cancelled because of heavy snow.) A tour which kicked off at Warrington on 14th September, ended with a Test match in Paris on 18th January - a total of 36 matches played, with 28 won, seven lost and one drawn. When they got home, those triumphant Kangaroos of 1963-64 were granted a tour bonus of £402 each to go with their £15 a week allowance paid throughout the four months away in Europe.

This was the last of the "daylight" tours, with only one match in addition to the first Test at Wembley played under floodlights - that was at Leigh. Other midweek games were on Wednesday or Thursday afternoons, and the fans of Featherstone and Castleford - if they managed to sneak an afternoon off - were the only two to see their clubs beat the Aussies.

1963 KANGAROOS IN ENGLAND

Warrington	won	28-20	20,090
Huddersfield	won	6-5	13,398
Yorkshire (Hull K.R.)	lost	5-11	10,324
Leeds	won	13-10	16,641
Lancashire (Wigan)	lost	11-13	15,068
St Helens	won	8-2	21,284
Featherstone Rovers	lost	17-23	7,898
Oldham	won	12-4	11,338
Leigh	won	33-7	9,625
Hull-Hull K.R. XIII	won	23-10	10,481
GT. BRITAIN (Wembley)	**won**	**28-2**	**13,946**
Rochdale Hornets	won	3-0	8,637
Hunslet	won	17-13	4,400
Wakefield Trinity	won	29-14	15,821
Cumberland (Workington)	won	21-0	8,229
Barrow	won	18-5	10,130
GT. BRITAIN (Swinton)	**won**	**50-12**	**30,833**
Castleford	lost	12-13	7,887
Wigan	won	18-10	11,746
Widnes	won	20-9	6,509
Swinton	drew	2-2	11,947
GT. BRITAIN (Leeds)	**lost**	**5-16**	**20,497**

KANGAROO TOURS

(Left) Don Fox on his was to a try for Featherstone Rovers as they beat the 1963 Australian touring team 23-17 in a thriller at Post Office Road. Fox is evading the Aussie tough-guy Noel Kelly as he crosses the line, watched closely by Rovers hooker Willis Fawley and the referee John Hebblethwaite. This Wednesday afternoon win is etched in the folklore of Featherstone Rovers.

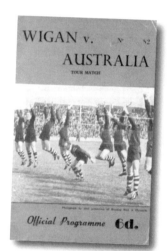

The second Kangaroo tour of the 'sixties saw the Australians arrive in a very different world to what they had known before. It was 1967, they would be playing under the four-tackle rule and, for the first time, the Aussies came to England defending the Ashes they had won on their previous tour four years earlier. The challenge of the 1966 Lions had been rebuffed (albeit narrowly) leaving a Kangaroo team captain-coached by Reg Gasnier to head to England confident that defeat was no longer a forgone conclusion for the Aussies.

They did manage to retain the Ashes, showing great resiliance in the face of injuries. Skipper Gasnier broke his leg in the first Test at Headingley, and when vice-captain Johnny Raper broke his cheekbone, second-rower "Pedro" Gallagher was left to captain Australia to a vital second Test equaliser played under lights at the White City in London. Many of the other tour fixtures were played under floodlights, notably at Belle Vue, Wakefield where a record Yorkshire County match crowd of almost 20,000 turned out - but, as a sign of the changing times in England, some of the club matches drew attendances that would have been unthinkably small on previous tours.

The 1967 Kangaroos were less successful overall than their 1963 counterparts, losing seven and drawing one of their 20 games in England. In France they played seven games, and lost the Test series, two-nil with one drawn.

1967 KANGAROOS IN ENGLAND

Warrington	won	16-7	11,642
Yorkshire (Wakefield)	lost	14-15	19,370
Hull K.R.	lost	15-27	11,252
Lancashire (Salford)	won	14-2	9,369
Wigan	lost	6-12	22,770
Rochdale H.	won	25-2	2,676
GT. BRITAIN (Leeds)	**lost**	**11-16**	**22,293**
St. Helens	lost	4-8	17,275
Wakefield T.	won	33-7	10,056
GT.BRITAIN (White City)	**won**	**17-11**	**17,445**
Castleford	lost	3-22	6,137
Oldham	won	18-8	3,174
Widnes	won	33-11	9,828
Barrow	drew	10-10	8,418
Cumberland (Workington)	lost	15-17	7,545
Swinton	won	12-9	5,640
Leeds	won	7-4	5,522
Halifax	won	22-2	5,285
Bradford N.	won	7-3	14,173
GT.BRITAIN (Swinton)	**won**	**11-3**	**13,615**

(Above) The 1967 Kangaroos, led by Reg Gasnier, before their opening tour match at Warrington.

Arthur Beetson on life with the Robins

The most memorable of all "guest" players from Australia during the 'sixties was the giant forward Arthur Beetson, who turned out for Hull K.R. in 1968 - Beetson played just 12 games for the Robins before breaking his leg on Christmas Day, but they still remember his stay vividly in East Hull, and so does Arthur himself.

(Above) **Arthur Beetson in one of his memorable games for Hull K.R. in 1968, this one against Featherstone Rovers at Craven Park with Vince Farrar coming across to try and tackle Arthur.**

My time at Hull K.R. was a wonderfully enjoyable one, although it was to finish badly. I loved England, loved the climate - which suited me, being a big bloke. I loved the football over there. I loved the social life. And I loved the people and admired their knowledge of Rugby League and passion for the game.

My fellow Aussie Jimmy Hall and I quickly became a source of amusement in Hull, because we'd go around in T-shirts, shorts and thongs (flip-flops), despite the first sharp bite of the English autumn.

I played only 12 games for Hull K.R., and was sent off in a couple of them, but in that short time I played some of the best football of my career. In successive games, against Featherstone and Castleford, I was named man-of-the-match.

My reputation as a pie-eater paled into insignificance with what some of the Rovers boys ate on the road trips. On match days, heading to some faraway ground across in Lancashire, our bus would pull up at a service place or a restaurant for lunch. It would be midday or so, with a match to be played at three o'clock, and my teammates would all pitch into the full baked dinner: veggies, potatoes and all the trimmings. Then they'd go for a walk and be ready for kick-off.

Leading into the Christmas period there was a string of games scheduled - four in eight days or something like that. Jimmy Hall and I added up all the pounds we'd be earning on top of our 10 pounds a week living allowance and came to the conclusion that we were going to be millionaires. But it all came unstuck, for me anyway, on a Christmas Day I won't forget.

On Christmas morning, traditionally, the two Hull sides met - Rovers (the Robins) and Hull F.C. (the Airlie Birds.) The game had an 11 am kick-off, to allow people to get home in time for Christmas lunch, and Jimmy and I were late, mainly due to the events of a big night out. Because we were hopelessly behind schedule arriving at the ground, I didn't do something that I always did before playing a match - strap my ankles.

We didn't get there until half an hour before kick-off and by then coach Colin Hutton, who was doubling as strapper that day, was panicking. He had two blokes from the "A" team stripped and ready to run on, and made it very plain that he was totally pissed off with us. His dissatisfaction was entirely understandable - this was the biggest game of the year for Hull K.R.; it didn't matter if we ran last in the comp., but we had to beat Hull !

There was barely time to get changed, but my early minutes of the game were like my Test debut in 1966 - I managed to put a couple of tries on to give us a flying start. I was going great guns. Then, 20 minutes into the match, in front of the grandstand, I was tackled awkwardly and hit the ground badly.

Colin Hutton was on the touchline as I lay there. "Bloody hell Arthur, this is no time to be fooling around," he yelled. "Get up and play the ball."

"Colin, I've done my leg," I called back at him. I struggled to my feet somehow and played the ball, but after that I couldn't move. I was gone. Late morning on that Christmas Day of 1968 they took me off and to the local hospital.

1960

WINNERS:
Challenge Cup: Wakefield Trinity.
Championship: Wigan.
Lancashire League: St.Helens.
Yorkshire League: Wakefield Trinity.
Lancashire Cup: St.Helens.
Yorkshire Cup: Wakefield Trinity.
County Championship: Lancashire.
Lance Todd Trophy: Tommy Harris (Hull).

* Great Britain win the World Cup again.
* The Queen attends R.L. Cup Final at Wembley.
* Wigan win Championship from fourth place.
* Murphy inspires Saints to Lancashire Cup.

(Above)
Alan Davies on his way to a try for Great Britain versus New Zealand in the 1960 World Cup.

Glorious sunshine greeted Her Majesty Queen Elizabeth as she attended the 1960 Rugby League Challenge Cup Final at Wembley, thus becoming only the second reigning monarch to do so as she followed in the footsteps of her late father, King George, who had been present at the 1948 Final. What the Queen saw was a sparkling display of open, attacking rugby provided by Wakefield Trinity and the gallant injury-hit runners-up Hull, before Trinity emerged winners by a record 38-5 scoreline. Spectacular tries by Ken Rollin, Neil Fox, Alan Skene, Keith Holliday and Fred Smith were like exhibition stuff from Wakefield as they announced their arrival as the team who would become the biggest name in Rugby League of the 'sixties. Glorious Wembley was in stark contrast to the wars of attrition Trinity had been forced to fight to get to the Cup Final, negotiating very determined opponents in tough conditions. They had the perfect general to show the way when the going was at its toughest in skipper Derek Turner, and "Rocky" was never more dominant than in Wakefield's epic quarter-final at Whitehaven.

(Above) **Suited, bruised and sitting on the bench together - Mick Sullivan and Alex Murphy after being sent off by referee Eric Clay for fighting each other in the 1960 top-four semi-final between Wigan and St.Helens.**
(Right) **Wakefield captain Derek Turned dives over for the vital score in the 1960 Cup quarter-final, with Whitehaven's Bill Holliday, Harry Hughes and Bill Smith in his wake.**

After lifting the Challenge Cup, Turner completed his year by being part of Great Britain's World Cup winning team, but his biggest disappointment was Wakefield's heavy defeat to Wigan in the Championship Final. In the space of a week, over 160,000 people attended the two end-of-season Finals in 1960 - leaving St.Helens to curse their luck in losing at home to Wigan in the top-four play-off. Saints had finished top, fully 13 points ahead of Wigan, only to see their rivals crowned as Champions.

World Cup winners paid £85 and no photo.

(*Above*) Australian centre Harry Wells tries to bamboozle the French defence in the opening 1960 World Cup match at Central Park, Wigan. A 20,000 crowd enjoyed a nail-biting encounter, most cheering for France as they lost by just one point to the Aussies.

Great Britain's World Cup winning team of 1960 made the grand total of £85 each from being victorious in the competition. The players were paid £20 for each of their three wins (over New Zealand, France and Australia), plus a bonus of £25 for winning the trophy. Two days after the World Cup deciding victory over Australia at Bradford, the Great Britain team returned to Odsal Stadium to play a "Rest of the World" composite team selected from the Aussies, Kiwis and French ranks. The British team won an entertaining celebration under the Odsal floodlights by 33 points to 27, and finally got their hands on the World Cup trophy the following day (Tuesday 11th October) at a reception for all the countries staged in Leeds by Jim Windsor. No photograph has ever been sighted of the Great Britain captain Eric Ashton being presented with the World Cup in 1960.

IN 1960

An 18-year-old amateur boxer from America, Cassius Clay, won a gold medal at the 1960 Olympics in Rome. He went on to become the world's most famous sportsman throughout the decade, later changing his name to Muhammad Ali.

Back in the U.K., National Service comes to an end as the last conscripts (including several Rugby League players) receive their call-up papers.

HITS HEARD ON THE TANNOY AT YOUR LOCAL R.L. GROUND
* *Apache* - The Shadows
* *Only the Lonely* - Roy Orbison
* *Cathy's Clown* - Everly Bros.
* *It's Now or Never* - Elvis
* *Chain Gang* - Sam Cooke

Wigan become the N.R.L. Champions for the ninth time

Wigan became Champions of the Northern Rugby League for the ninth time after they convincingly beat Wakefield Trinity, 27-3, at Odsal Stadium on 21st May 1960. Although Wigan had only just scraped into the top-four ahead of Featherstone Rovers, they showed their quality by beating league leaders St.Helens before 33,000 at Knowsley Road in the semi-final and then stunning Cup winners Wakefield in the Championship Final. Trinity started in their Wembley form as Ken Rollin sent winger Fred Smith over after just two minutes play - and it took a couple of Fred Griffiths penalties to peg them back before Billy Boston scored bang on half-time to give

(*Above*) Billy Boston touches down for a try as Wigan beat Wakefield in the Championship Final of 1960. Wigan winger Frank Halliwell celebrates Billy's try.

Wigan a 9-3 interval lead. In the second-half Wigan cut loose with four more tries by Eric Ashton (2), Bill Sayer and Boston again. Wigan coach Joe Egan had played a masterstroke by switiching Billy Boston to centre to counter the physical power of Neil Fox, with Eric Ashton and David Bolton forming a new half-back partnership. In the event, Boston's job was made easier when Fox injured the knee of his goal-kicking leg in the thirteenth minute, leaving him a passenger for the rest of the game. A record Championship Final crowd of 83,190 provided receipts of £14,914 on that memorable day at Odsal.

1961

WINNERS:
Challenge Cup: St.Helens.
Championship: Leeds.
Lancashire League: Swinton.
Yorkshire League: Leeds.
Lancashire Cup: St.Helens.
Yorkshire Cup: Wakefield Trinity.
County Championship: Cumberland.
Lance Todd Trophy: Dick Huddart (St.Helens).

* First ever Championship win for Leeds.
* Vollenhoven's try in Wembley scorcher.
* Great Britain beats Kiwis in Test series.
* The first Fijians arrive at Rochdale.

(Above)
Wembley glory for St.Helens - wearing the red vee for the very first time - as they beat Wigan 12-6 in the Challenge Cup Final of 1961. This quartet of happy Saints are: Don Vines, Mick Sullivan, Alex Murphy and Cliff Watson.

It was hard to believe that Leeds, despite being one of the game's biggest and wealthiest clubs, had never, ever won the Championship. All that changed in 1961 when the years of careful team-building put in by football manager Joe Warham, and before him Ken Dalby, came to fruition as the Loiners - at last - held the famous trophy to signify season-long superiority.

After finishing top of the table with 60 points, five ahead of second-placed Warrington, Leeds beat St.Helens 11-4 at Headingley in the top-four semi-final to qualify for the Championship Final. The Wire were their opponents after they overcame third-placed Swinton 13-5 in their semi-final. The showdown came at Odsal Stadium with a crowd of 52,300 present to see Leeds finally win the title by comprehensively beating their Lancastrian opponents 25-10.

The game's highest profile reporter, Eddie Waring described Leeds thus: "Brilliantly led by that enigma of Rugby League football, Lewis Jones, they methodically, emphatically, crushed Warrington. Rarely has any pack monopolised a game as did the Leeds "terrible six" (to steal a Hunslet phrase."

(Right)
Mick Sullivan hurdles to avoid his colleague Alex Murphy as Great Britain won the deciding Test match of the Autumn 1961 series versus New Zealand. The British victory by 35 points to 19, sealed an entertaining series with the Kiwis. The visitors had won the opening Test at Leeds 29-11, with Great Britain coming back to win the second Test at Bradford 23-10.

There was no official "man of the match" award in the Championship Final in those days but, had there been one, Eddie Waring was sure it should go to the Leeds hooker Barry Simms, a view echoed by all involved with the Loiners' camp that day. Simms had secured plenty of possession from the scrums and produced some brilliant open play in the loose, to lead the way for the rest of his pack: Dennis Goodwin, Jack Fairbank, Brian Shaw, Trevor Whitehead and Don Robinson.

The running of Derek Hallas and Ken Thornett in the backs has been majestic, but the man who pulled the strings was captain Lewis Jones. It proved to be the crowning glory in the sometimes controversial career of the Welsh star, much beloved at Headingley and revered in the club's history.

N̲o other Wembley Cup Finals are remembered so vividly for one individual try as much as the 1961 Final is for the score by St.Helens winger Tom Van Vollenhoven. His inter-passing with centre Ken Large which covered most of the length of the pitch is unforgettable for all of the 94,672 spectators present at Wembley that day plus the millions of television viewers who watched it huddled around their small black and white sets. Saints beat Wigan 12-6 on a very hot day - Dick Huddart reckons he lost a stone in weight due to the heat - but it didn't stop the rampaging second-rower powering his way to the Lance Todd Trophy.

(Above)
The moment of glory for Leeds as skipper Lewis Jones raises the Championship trophy aloft at Odsal stadium in May 1961.

A note of trivia from the 1961 Cup Final, was the referee Mr. Tom Watkinson the last to officiate at Wembley wearing a blazer? The defeat had more serious repercussions for Wigan whose Board of Directors were so disappointed at losing to St.Helens that they sacked their coach Joe Egan. Joe didn't take long to bounce back, he moved to Widnes and three years later returned to Wembley to win the Cup with a Chemics team captained by none other than Vince Karalius.

(Right)
Vince Karalius leads Saints down the Wembley steps with the Cup in 1961. Immediately behind Vinty are Austin Rhodes, Tom Van Vollenhoven and Ken Large. The clash between the two South West Lancashire giants, Wigan and Saints, had captured the imagination like few previous Cup Finals.

IN 1961

A year when Wigan's most famous native, George Formby died at the age of 57 - and its most famous signing, Ellery Hanley, was born. So too was Barack Obama, Frank Bruno and Eddie Murphy.
This was also the year that Tottenham Hotspur became the first football team in the 20th Century to win the double

HITS HEARD ON THE TANNOY AT YOUR LOCAL R.L. GROUND
* *Runaway* - Del Shannon
* *The Wanderer* - Dion
* *Halfway to Paradise* - Billy Fury
* *Walkin' Back to Happiness* - Helen Shapiro
* *Please Mr. Postman* - The Marvellettes

1962

WINNERS:
Challenge Cup: Wakefield Trinity.
Championship: Huddersfield.
Lancashire League: Wigan.
Yorkshire League: Wakefield Trinity.
Lancashire Cup: St.Helens.
Yorkshire Cup: Hunslet.
County Championship: Yorkshire.
Lance Todd Trophy: Neil Fox (Wakefield Trinity).

* Wakefield just miss out on "All Four Cups."
* A Championship title for Huddersfield.
* Great Britain's brilliant Ashes win down-under.
* The arrival of Two Divisions.

(Above)
Neil Fox dives over to score for England in an 18-6 win over France at Headingley in November 1962. The victory was in stark contrast to the three full Tests between Great Britain and France in 1962, all won by the French.

What a game of contrasts Rugby League was in 1962. Whilst at home in England it seemed to be beset by constant bickering over things like the rules, the fixture format and how to rid itself of foul play and negative tactics - all brought on, no doubt, by the financial pressures being felt due to falling attendance figures in some quarters - on the other side of the world in Australia the Great Britain touring team proceeded to produce some of the most rip-roaring, skilful attacking football the world of rugby had ever seen, to retain the Ashes in spectacular style.

The old adage that "there's nowt wrong with the rules if teams play with a positive attitude" had never rung more true and it was hard to believe that, in four year's time, the need would be felt to introduce a four-tackle rule. Alex Murphy was the star of the tour, but another scrum-half left at home, Tommy Smales, was most unlucky to miss out on Lions selection after leading his Huddersfield team to victory in the Championship Final and a close defeat in the Cup Final at Wembley. Fartown's opponents in both those Finals were a Wakefield Trinity team in their prime. With Derek Turner, Neil Fox and Harold Poynton also to go on and play key roles in the Ashes victory, Trinity had looked all set to win "All Four Cups" before Tommy Smales and his men spiked their guns at Odsal. Huddersfield came from fourth place to win the Championship and it was to be the last of the traditional top-four play-offs to decide the title as Two Divisions were being introduced in the 1962-63 season.

Fartown fans stampede

(Above) **Remarkable scenes at Odsal Stadium during the 1962 Championship Final as Huddersfield fans invaded the pitch following the try by their team captain Tommy Smales which sealed the victory over Wakefield Trinity to take the title back to Fartown. The Wakefield full-back Gerry Round is on the floor amid the stampede of Huddersfield supporters eager to mob their heroes.**

(Right)
The French half-back Louis Verges breaks from the back of a scrum as Great Britain were beaten in Perpignan in March 1962. Captain Jean Barthe locks the scrum.

Whilst all eyes were on the Great Britain team in the spring of 1962, ahead of their tour to Australia, it was France who went surging forward by winning both home and away Tests as well as opening a brand new modern ground in Perpignan. The Gilbert Brutus stadium staged a Test match for the first time on 11th March 1962, in which France beat Great Britain 23-13, to follow up their earlier 20-15 win at Wigan. France had one of their strongest ever sides, with brilliant half-backs in Gilbert Benausse and "little Louis" Verges and the dynamic full-back Andre Carrere playing behind a monster pack including Bescos, Quaglio, Ailleres and Barthe.

Tom Mitchell's dramatic call saved the 1962 Lions tour

Tom Mitchell's dramatic, and ultimately successful, bid to save the 1962 Lions tour to Australia, which had been called off, was described at the time as a landmark of Rugby League history. Tom was the Council chairman during the 1961-62 seasons when a serious rift developed between Great Britain and Australia over the division of tour receipts. The two countries were divided over a matter of 5%. Britain wanted a 65-35% split of the tour takings, but Australia rejected this and offered 60-40, after starting off with a 50-50 demand.

Neither side would budge and, in November 1961, it was announced that the tour would not take place. As chairman, Tom Mitchell had a great deal of personal anxiety during this period. Was the work of past touring pioneers to be cast to the winds? Would the tour threads ever be picked up again? Would the World Cup idea be abandoned? These were among the questions that prompted him to book a radio-telephone call in the early hours of the morning to his counterpart in Sydney, Mr. Bill Buckley, with whom he had had excellent relations on the 1958 tour. As a result of that call (Tom sat up all night waiting for it) it was made clear that the tour's financial success was guaranteed because of the large attendances in Australia and increased admission prices.

Tom Mitchell - saved the tour.

Tom Mitchell firmly believed that the 1962 tour (and the prospect of future tours) mattered more than the 5% difference - an estimated £2,000. He wrote a letter to each member of the Rugby League Council setting out the facts as he saw them, and following a special Council meeting in Leeds on 23rd November 1961, the newspaper headlines were able to state: *"The tour goes on!"*

It must be remembered that the Council's decision (after three lengthy meetings) to call the tour off, had been a unanimous one. Mitchell had to use his persuasive powers to the full to even get the matter discussed again, as a two thirds majority was required to do so. What the Council did not know was that he had risked his position as chairman by telling Bill Buckley that, as far as he was concerned, the tour was still ON.

The voting was 24 to 4 in favour of sending a Lions team to Australia, with the proviso that Australia's offer was accepted as a temporary agreement to cover the 1962 tour and the Kangaroos' 1963 visit to England. Tom had won his point and earned the gratitude of thousands of Rugby League enthusiasts in doing so.

Any doubts about the financial result were removed when the tour produced a record profit for Great Britain. Bill Buckley had kept his promise!

1963

WINNERS:
Challenge Cup: Wakefield Trinity.
Championship: Swinton.
Lancashire Cup: St.Helens.
Yorkshire Cup: Halifax.
Division Two Championship: Hunslet.
Western Division: Workington Town.
Eastern Division: Hull Kingston Rovers.
County Championship: Cumberland.
Lance Todd Trophy: Harold Poynton (Wakefield T.).

* The big winter freeze causes fixture backlog.
* Swinton the first past the post Champions.
* Australia finally wins the Ashes in England.
* South Africa makes its first tour.

(Above)
Vince Karalius in his last appearance for Great Britain at Swinton in November 1963. It was the day Rugby League history was made as Australia hammered injury-hit opponents 50-8 to win the Ashes on English soil for the first time.

It would be difficult to find a more dramatic and action-packed year in the whole history of Rugby League than 1963. It came in wrapped up in the big freeze as the worst winter weather since 1947 caused weeks of postponements amid frantic efforts by some clubs to get pitches thawed out. Widnes sprayed chemicals on Naughton Park which did allow some matches to be played, and Leeds got to work on installing undersoil heating The 1962-63 season was extended and no fewer than 106 league games were crammed into an added period of 1st May to 1st June, saying much for the fortitude of the Rugby League clubs and their players that they were able to complete all league fixtures as well as the Challenge Cup campaign.

Swinton were crowned as the Rugby League Champions - the inaugural winners of the new First Division. There was no top-four play-off anymore, and the Lions captained by Albert Blan were first past the post winners, as in the Football League, and very popular winners they were as the "swinging sixties" emerged in the north west of England. That same style was echoed by Wakefield Trinity, winning their third Wembley Final in four years. Trinity had two of a new generation of South Africans on their wings at Wembley - Colin Greenwood and Gert Coetzer - as more and more attention was being focussed on their homeland and the attempts to establish Rugby League there.

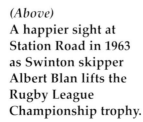

(Above)
A happier sight at Station Road in 1963 as Swinton skipper Albert Blan lifts the Rugby League Championship trophy.

At last there were genuine hopes that a new force in international Rugby League was about to emerge, and the South Africans made their first tour to Australia and New Zealand in 1963. Alas, when their players returned home they found the fledgling League code under enormous pressure from the Rugby Union authorities and, denied access to grounds and other public support, they found it impossible to carry on. Much more drama was to follow on the international stage in the autumn of 1963 as the Kangaroos came on

(Right)
Wigan followed the example of Rochdale Hornets when they signed Fijian star Kia Bose in 1963. But Kia got a huge shock when he arrived at Central Park in the middle of the big freeze to find the ground frozen solid as workman with pneumatic drills tried to break the ice.

tour to England and France, and became the first Australian team to win the Ashes over here. They did it spectacularly, with thrashings at Wembley (under floodlights) and on a famous November afternoon at Station Road which has gone down in history as "the Swinton massacre." The most positive story of 1963 was Blackpool's opening of their brand new ground Borough Park, the first new stadium to be created in British Rugby League since Workington built Derwent Park. And the saddest tale was the demise of Bradford Northern who withdrew from the League in December 1963.

IN 1963

Daily Mirror **KENNEDY ASSASSINATED**
Jackie spattered with blood

The headline that said it all - 1963's most infamous event happened in Dallas, Texas on 22nd November.

HITS HEARD ON THE TANNOY AT YOUR LOCAL R.L. GROUND
* *Be My Baby* - The Ronettes
* *From Me to You* - The Beatles
* *He's So Fine* - The Chiffons
* *Da Doo Ron Ron* - The Crystals
* *She Loves You* - The Beatles

Three ordered off in Headingley third Test rough-house

EDDIE WARING'S VIEW FROM HEADINGLEY

Three players sent off ... one carried off on a stretcher ... a verbal attack on referee Eric Clay by Aussie team manager Jack Lynch ... this was the third Test and a sorry finish to the 1963 Kangaroos' tour.

Sent off were two Australians, Brian Hambly (17 minutes) and Barry Muir (56 minutes), and Britain's Cliff Watson (49 minutes), Five minutes from the end Australian winger Ken Irvine was a stretcher case with damaged ribs.

The only good thing that came out of the brawl was the fact that Britain, with ten changes and six new caps after the Swinton debacle, recaptured a little of their international prestige. The new boys played a decisive role in the victory. John

(Pictured) Referee Eric Clay steps in to break up Britain's Ken Roberts and Australia's Brian Hambly in one of the many 1963 third Test brawls.

Ward, the young Castleford hooker, celebrated his first international by winning the scrums and scoring the first try in the 21st minute following smart handling byDon Fox and Alan Buckley. Loose-forward Fox, playing his first Test in that position, contributed seven points to the victory.

Two of Great Britain's four tries, scored by wingers John Stopford and Geoff Smith, came from high kicks by Dave Bolton in what were obviously planned moves. In response to the vitriolic criticism by Australian manager Lynch, referee Eric Clay commented: *"I did my job as I saw fit and as far as I am concerned my conscience is perfectly clear."*

Great Britain beat Australia 16-5, to finish the series 2-1.

1964

WINNERS:
Challenge Cup: Widnes.
Championship: Swinton.
Lancashire Cup: St.Helens.
Yorkshire Cup: Wakefield Trinity.
Division Two Championship: Oldham.
Western Division: St.Helens.
Eastern Division: Halifax.
County Championship: Yorkshire.
Lance Todd Trophy: Frank Collier (Widnes).

* Widnes take the Merseybeat to Wembley.
* Swinton's second successive Championship.
* Oldham's Wembley dreams shattered again.
* The rise of Hull K.R. and Classy Cas'.

(Above)
Widnes show the Cup on their lap of honour at Wembley after a 13-5 victory over Hull K.R. A try by international Frank Myler in the 56th minute had given the Chemics the edge after the Robins, in their first Wembley Final, had pushed them all the way.

In a year when the Merseybeat was in full swing it was fitting that Widnes should take centre stage on the game's biggest occasion, winning the 1964 Challenge Cup Final, captained by Vince Karalius. The Chemics emerged triumphant after an incredible marathon Cup campaign which featured more draws and replays than ever before. Widnes featured in five replays to get to Wembley, and their opponent s Hull K.R. in three. It seemed the more times teams had to replay, the bigger the crowds got - among the best figures were 31,752 at Central Park for Wigan versus Swinton the first round, followed by 26,891 at Station Road for the Wednesday afternoon replay.

Albert Blan and his Lions were hot tips for Wembley, but fell after two replays against Widnes. Consolation for Swinton was a second successive Championship title to see them dominate the game's short lived Two Divisions era. The clubs voted to scrap the new league format in February 1964, just half way through its three-year experiment - it seemed ironic that it proved such a failure at the same time as Cup tie crowds were booming. Two new names were beginning to be mentioned among the game's elite with the steady rise of both Hull Kingston Rovers and Castleford. With Colin Hutton at the helm as

(Right)
First signs began to emerge in 1964 that Castleford were about to become a new force in the game. They were unlucky not to make it to Wembley after a good Cup run which included a dominant win away at Whitehaven in the second round. In that game, we can see Castleford's Geoff Ward and John Sheridan battling for a ball on the floor with Whiutehaven forwards Les Moore and Frank Moss.

Why top league players train on BOVRIL

Many leading Rugby League players drink hot Bovril daily right through the season. They find it a big help in keeping them at the top of their form. **League players must keep fit.** Bovril keeps them fit. It provides | warmth and nourishment and helps them give their best for the full eighty minutes of every match—and Bovril is very low in fattening calories. That's why the men in the team drink Bovril—and they thoroughly enjoy it. You will too!

Bovril for fitness without fatness

(Above) **Action from the 1964 Cup Final at Wembley as Hull K.R. forward Eric Palmer is tackled by Widnes prop Wally Hurstfield and captain Vince Karalius with the Chemics' hooker George Kemel looking on.**

(Above) **This advert, which appeared in the Cup Final programme of 1964, revealed the secret for success in Rugby League. There were no special diets or muscle-building supplements back then, it was all down to a mug of Bovril - for fitness without fatness.**

coach, the Robins had emerged from the shadow of their Hull F.C. neighbours in the 'fifties to reach Wembley for the first time. Captain Harry Poole was a key figure in this rise of the Rovers. Another great "phoenix-like" achievement in 1964 was the rebirth of Bradford Northern - the game had been shocked by their demise mid-way through the 1963-64 season, but when they made their return in August 1964, the crowd of 13,542 for their opening match at Odsal versus Hull K.R. was around 2,000 more than Northern had drawn for their entire season of 13 league fixtures in 1962-63.

Not so happy were Oldham who had seen their long held dream of going to Wembley come so tantalisingly close in 1964. Despite being a Second Division side at the time, Oldham had drawn 5-all with Hull K.R. in the semi-final, and were leading 17-14 in the replay after that game went into extra time, only for it to be abandoned due to the light fading. In the second replay Hull K.R. prevailed, leaving Oldham to carry on dreaming of what might have been. 1964 also saw the retirement of Brian Bevan, the game's greatest try-scorer, after a final fling at Blackpool Borough.

(Right)
Oldham's Charlie Bott and Geoff Robinson get tangled up with Hull K.R. defenders in the infamous abandoned Cup semi-final replay at Station Road.

IN 1964

These lads, who invented the "Swinging Sixties," were rumoured to have spent their Saturday afternoons at Knotty Ash cheering on Liverpool City before dashing off to the Cavern.

HITS HEARD ON THE TANNOY AT YOUR LOCAL R.L. GROUND
* *Needles and Pins* - The Searchers
* *Something Good* - Herman's Hermits
* *Bits and Pieces* - Dave Clark Five
* *Pretty Woman* - Roy Orbison
* *Downtown* - Petula Clark

1965

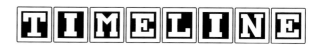

WINNERS:
Challenge Cup: Wigan.
Championship: Halifax.
Lancashire League: St.Helens.
Yorkshire League: Castleford.
Lancashire Cup: Warrington.
Yorkshire Cup: Bradford Northern.
County Championship: Cumberland
Lance Todd Trophy: Brian Gabbitas (Hunslet)
and Ray Ashby (Wigan).

* *Hunslet's uplifting display at Wembley.*
* *Halifax win the Championship from seventh.*
* *Castleford the first Floodlit trophy winners.*
* *French farce holds up Test match at Swinton.*

(Above)
Wembley brought the traditional after-match interview by the BBC's David Coleman for Wigan's captain-coach Eric Ashton in 1965. It was Eric's and Wigan's third Wembley Final to date in the 'sixties and their first win there, as Hunslet were beaten 20-16 in a very entertaining match.

Rugby League basked in the glory of a superbly entertaining Challenge Cup Final in 1965 between Wigan and Hunslet, which drew praise far and wide for the game. Wigan won the trophy, which was much relief for a club which had suffered defeat at Wembley in 1961 and '63, but it was great to see Hunslet back in the big time with their team made up almost exclusively of local juniors (Welsh winger John Griffiths being the only non Yorkshireman.) The exciting action from Wembley was telecast in America, with the BBC's Eddie Waring stating he truly believed Rugby League now had a big opportunity to attract a new audience across the Atlantic.

More joy was felt by Halifax, surprise winners of the Championship as the Northern Rugby League returned to a one division format, only now with a top-16 play off to decide the Champions. And the new Bradford Northern, only one year into their "reformation," fulfilled Chairman Joe Phillips's prophecy that they would win a major trophy within three seasons, claiming the Yorkshire Cup after victory over Hunslet in the Final. Northern had a new talisman in their scrum-half Tommy Smales, whose success in leading Bradford saw him selected as Great Britain's captain in the 1965 Test series versus New Zealand.

The Kiwis arrived for their tour in England as the unofficial world "champions" after becoming the first winners of the Courtney Goodwill Trophy. This was decided after compiling the records of all matches played by the four Test playing nations over a five year period, March 1960 to March 1965, and the New Zealanders came out on top with a 66.6% ratio. Australia were second with 62.5%, Great Britain third with 50% and France fourth with only 31%. Interestingly, the Kiwis had played just 18 fixtures to decide their percentage, whereas France had played 29. Despite holding the giant Courtney Trophy, the 1965 Kiwis were comfortably beaten by both Great Britain and France. Not so good from the French was the embarrassing scene caused for the game, in full view of a national

Millward makes first mark

Our young startler, ROGER MILLWARD, after being the T.V. star of amateur football, and then a prolific try and goal scorer in the Senior Competition, has been the talking point in senior football in recent weeks. Given that little bit of luck and freedom from injury, there is no doubt that he will eventually make his mark in representative football.

Roger Millward

(Above) **Some prophetic words in this cutting from the Castleford programme for their match versus York at Wheldon Road on 11th October 1965.**

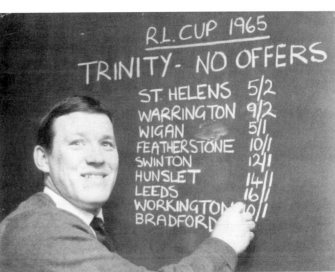

(Above) French captain Marcel Bescos weeps in the Station Road dressing room after being sent off by referee Dennis Davies in the 1965 Test match. The picture shows him being comforted by Jacques Reynes, the secretary of the French R.L. Federation and one of the substitute players that day, Patrick Carrias.

(Above)
Neil Fox had become a Bookmaker in Wakefield but, of course, was not able to offer any odds on his own Trinity team when the Challenge Cup came around in 1965. Perhaps that was no bad thing, as Wakefield were beaten by Hunslet in the semi-final.

audience on live television, in the Test match at Swinton in January, 1965, when their captain Marcel Bescos refused to leave the field after being sent off by referee D.T.H. Davies. Bescos prompted his team to walk off and there was a delay of seven minutes before order was restored and play resumed ... with Bescos left on the sidelines.

Floodlights were bringing a new dimension to Rugby League in 1965, and in the autumn the BBC launched their their Floodlit Trophy. Castleford emerged as the first winners of the trophy, beating St.Helens at Knowsley Road 4-nil in the first ever Final. Many clubs were rushing to get lights installed so they could join the revolution.

Halifax new style champions

Halifax confounded all the odds to win the Rugby League Championship in 1965, after winning through to the Final from seventh place in the new style top-16 play-offs. After beating Leeds, Featherstone and Castleford to get to the Final, Halifax shocked the league leaders and favourites, St.Helens, to win 15-7 at Station Road.

That occasion saw the introduction of a new award, to the man of the match in the Championship Final, in memory of Harry Sunderland, the great Australian journalist and Rugby League visionary, who had died in January 1964. The very first winner was Halifax second-row-forward Terry Fogerty

(Above) Terry Fogerty, first Harry Sunderland Trophy winner in 1965.

IN 1965

In January 1965, Sir Winston Churchill died at the age of 90, and in the following month we also said farewell to Ulverston's finest, Stan Laurel, the British half of Laurel and Hardy.
In sport Stanley Matthews played his last top-flight football game at the age of 50.

"Evening all ..." Dixon of Dock Green looks forward to his best day of the year, on duty with those friendly folk at the Rugby League Cup Final at Wembley.

HITS HEARD ON THE TANNOY AT YOUR LOCAL R.L. GROUND
* *Mr Tambourine Man* - The Byrds
* *I'm Alive* - The Hollies
* *I Got You Babe* - Sonny and Cher
* *It's Not Unusual* - Tom Jones
* *Ticket To Ride* - The Beatles

1966

WINNERS:
Challenge Cup: St.Helens.
Championship: St.Helens.
Lancashire League: St.Helens.
Yorkshire League: Wakefield Trinity.
Lancashire Cup: Wigan.
Yorkshire Cup: Hull Kingston Rovers.
County Championship: Cumberland
Lance Todd Trophy: Len Killeen (St.Helens).

* *Great Britain robbed in Ashes thriller.*
* *St.Helens win the Cup and League Double.*
* *Alex Murphy turns down tour selection.*
* *Four tackle rule introduced to Rugby League.*

(Above)
Ian Brooke, supported by Alan Buckley, on the attack for Great Britain in the third Test of the 1966 Ashes series in Australia.

(Below)
Saints' Wembley joy as Alex Murphy hugs Tommy Bishop after his try in the 1966 Cup Final, with Len Killeen, Billy Benyon and John Warlow.

If historians of the rules of Rugby League want to look back on the significant changes in the game on the field of play, 1966 will always be the seminal year after the four-tackle rule was introduced. Finally, those who had long sought a method of stopping teams hogging the ball (with R.F.L. secretary Bill Fallowfield always leading the way) had got what they wanted as the new rule was introduced three months into the 1966-67 season in October '66. This followed a brief trial in the televised Floodlit Trophy games. To some, it was a revolution bringing back a new age of more open play, to others it was a shambles of frustration, panic kicking (including a flood of drop-goal attempts) and countless scrums. But the new rule was here to stay.

Even before then, some experienced commentators were beginning to question whether specialist hookers and heavyweight props would still have a part to play in the game, following the introduction of a new rule in August 1966 where a second tap-penalty was allowed after a penalty kick to touch, rather than a scrum. This rule, which originally was the brainchild of former Great Britain captain and coach Jim Brough, had been rushed through as a reaction to the tactics of St.Helens (perceived or otherwise) in their 1966 Cup Final win over Wigan. Critics suggested that Saints captain Alex Murphy had his team go deliberately offside at Wembley when Wigan were in possession, knowing that they had to kick for touch (tap penalties being banned at the time) and then form a scrum. And, without a recognised hooker due to Colin Clarke being suspended, the Saints vastly experienced number nine Bill Sayer (ex-Wigan) would shovel out the ball. St.Helens won the game comfortably, 21-2, and it was a shame that those accusations about Murphy's tactics should take some of the gloss of the Saints magnificent achievement of winning the double in 1966, and going threequarters of the way to winning "All Four Cups."

South African winger Len Killeen was the star of the 1966 Wembley Final, with a magnificent exhibition of goal-kicking, but you just couldn't keep his captain, Alex Murphy, out of the news in 1966. Playing in his new position of centre, Alex was selected for what would have been this third Lions tour, but withdrew from the squad claiming he couldn't spare time from his joinery business. The captaincy had been awarded to the uncapped Harry Poole, and not Murphy, and the controversies continued when experienced centres - and potential captains - Eric Ashton and Neil Fox subsequently turned down invitations to join the touring team after intially being over-looked. The 1966 Lions left a host of good players at home in what was one of the most overtly political of international team selections but, in the event, put up a good show in trying to win back the Ashes lost at home in 1963.

With Harry Poole and his vice-captain Ken Gowers injured for the first Test, the most experienced tourist Brian Edgar took over the captaincy, which he retained for all three Tests even when Gowers was back in the team. Edgar led his men from the front and, after winning the first Test in Sydney, they found themselves the victims of some highly controversial refereeing decisions in the other two Tests as the Australians scaped home to victory.

The accounts from the 1966 tour showed that total receipts were over £25,000 down on the 1962 tour, resulting in the players' bonus being well below the record £572 per man paid in 1962. But the Rugby Football League continued to be generous in its loans to clubs for ground improvements, mostly floodlights, but they also approved a loan of £20,000 to Liverpool City to aid the building of their new ground for their pending move to Huyton.

(Above)
Brian Edgar, the Workington Town forward who made a record equalling third Lions tour in 1966, and captained Great Britain in all three Ashes Tests in Australia.

Last of the St.George dynasty

In Australian Rugby League, 1966 saw the incredible run of Premierships for the St.George club extend to 11 consecutive years, following their 23-4 victory over Balmain in the Sydney Grand Final. Little did anyone know it would be the last of the dynasty as, the following year, St.George were finally beaten. Pictured *(above)* celebrating their 1966 success are happy St.George players Dick Huddart, Ian Walsh and Brian Clay (wearing a Balmain jersey.) Huddart had just become the first Englishman to play in a Sydney Grand Final, a record he shared with David Bolton who played for Balmain in that same match in 1966.

Whilst Brian Edgar was leading Great Britain in the Ashes series in Australia, on home soil the summer of 1966 belonged to Bobby Moore *(above)* and the England football team, who won the World Cup, beating West Germany in an epic and eventful Final at Wembley.

HITS HEARD ON THE TANNOY AT YOUR LOCAL R.L. GROUND
* *Sha-la-la-la-le* - The Small Faces
* *Keep on Runnin'* - Spencer Davis Group
* *I'm a Believer* - The Monkees
* *Good Vibrations* - The Beach Boys
* *Reach Out I'll be There* - The Four Tops

1967

WINNERS:
Challenge Cup: Featherstone Rovers.
Championship: Wakefield Trinity.
Lancashire League: St.Helens.
Yorkshire League: Leeds.
Lancashire Cup: St.Helens.
Yorkshire Cup: Hull Kingston Rovers.
County Championship: Lancashire.
Lance Todd Trophy: Carl Dooler (Featherstone R.)

* Wakefield Trinity win first ever Championship.
* Featherstone and Barrow meet at Wembley.
* Australia retains the Ashes in a snowstorm.
* Sunday matches allowed in Rugby League.

(Above)
Featherstone Rovers captain Malcolm Dixon meets Prince Philip before the 1967 Cup Final.

(Below)
Castleford and Bradford Northern were top ten clubs in 1966-67 and in their match at Odsal in March 1967, Johnny Walker dives over for a Cas' try, supported by Keith Hepworth.

The Challenge Cup Final of 1967 between lowly placed Barrow and Featherstone had a joyous charm about it, between two clubs who - looking at the league table - might hardly have expected to be going Wembley that year. Her Majesty the Queen attended her second Rugby League Cup Final and must have enjoyed her afternoon out in the Middlesex sunshine as Featherstone won the Cup for the first time in their history.

In sharp contrast, the Championship Final was cut and thrust, hard and tight, played in the rain at Headingley as Wakefield Trinity and St.Helens fought out a 7-all draw. The replay, four days later on a Wednesday night at Swinton, drew a 33,537 crowd to see Trinity achieve their Holy Graill of the Championship trophy. Harold Poynton was the skipper who achieved what all those great Trinity captains before him, including names like Jonty Parkin and Derek Turner, had been unable to do. Wakefield won the replay 21-9, with Widnesian scrum-half Ray Owen winning the Harry Sunderland trophy.

1967 had that special buzz as a Kangaroo tour year and it was a new experience for the Australians to find their midweek matches now being played under floodlights. After winning the first Test at Headingley, Great Britain missed a golden opportunity to regain the Ashes in the second rubber played at the White City in London. The Aussies were weakened by injuries but achieved an heroic win and, when the sides met for the decider at Swinton, there was only one winner. Australia adapted far better to the frozen ground and blizzard conditions and sealed the Ashes 11-3.

1967 saw another innovation to English Rugby League which was to play a major part in its future, when the inaugural Sunday games were allowed at first team professional level in December. They immediately saw bigger crowds.

Rovers' Wembley delight

(*Above*) Referee Eric Clay is right on the spot as Arnold Morgan scores for Featherstone at Wembley in 1967, beating Barrow defenders Mick Sanderson and Ray Hopwood - with Rovers captain Malcolm Dixon making sure the referee has seen the touchdown. Featherstone and Barrow produced an excellent Cup Final which belied their relatively low league positions - Barrow finished 15th and Featherstone 20th. It showed that the Cup could still produce the romance of small town clubs going to Wembley, with Rovers beating Yorkshire rivals Bradford, Wakefield and Castleford to get there.

Leigh the first on colour telly

The first Rugby League match to be televised in colour was in the 1967-68 season, when Leigh beat Wigan in the semi-final of the BBC Floodlit Trophy. The match was played at Knowsley Road, St.Helens and the second-half broadcast live on BBC 2. Leigh went on to play Castleford in the Final, losing 8-5. In the Leigh team in those games was centre Mick Collins, a stalwart at Hilton Park throughout the 'sixties after signing from Waterloo Rugby Union alongside Mick Murphy in 1963.

(*Above*) Leigh's Mick Collins - played in 1967.

IN 1967

The "Summer of Love" was happening, but there wasn't much sign of it in the Rugby League towns of Lancashire and Yorkshire. "Z Cars" was about as exotic as it got ... with Jock Wear playing for (Liverpool) City Rugby League Club, P.C. Graham turning out in later years to be Colin Welland, and Inspector Barlow now doubling as Shaun McRae. At Wembley, none of those lads from Featherstone had flowers in their hair.

HITS HEARD ON THE TANNOY AT YOUR LOCAL R.L. GROUND
* *A Whiter Shade of Pale* - Procul Harum
* *Everlasting Love* - Love Affair
* *Silence Is Golden* - The Tremeloes
* *Light My Fire* - The Doors
* *San Francisco* - Scott McKenzie

1968

WINNERS:
Challenge Cup: Leeds.
Championship: Wakefield Trinity.
Lancashire League: Warrington.
Yorkshire League: Leeds.
Lancashire Cup: St.Helens.
Yorkshire Cup: Leeds.
County Championship: Yorkshire.
Lance Todd Trophy: Don Fox (Wakefield Trinity).

* Australia wins the World Cup.
* Wembley's infamous Watersplash Final.
* Wakefield Trinity retain the Championship.
* Farewell to Tom Van Vollenhoven.

(Above)
The curtain came down on Billy Boston's career with Wigan at the end of April 1968. No player was more of a Rugby League icon, in Wigan and further afield, than Billy. He had a testimonial match at Central Park in July 1968, and answered Blackpool's call before hanging up his boots for good.

Mick Clark at the 1968 World Cup.

Forever remembered as the "Watersplash Final,"1968 saw one of the most dramatic moments in Rugby League's history. A missed conversion with the last kick of the game, saw Leeds win the Challenge Cup and Wakefield Trinity's hopes of a double slip agonisingly away. Trinity already had the Championship in the bag when they arrived at Wembley but, with the most debatable of obstruction tries awarded to Leeds, and then that cruel goal miss by Don Fox, they knew fate was against them that day.

It was a year to remember for Mick Clark who lifted the Cup as Leeds captain at Wembley. Mick, who had already played at Wembley for Huddersfield back in 1962, was called into the Great Britain team for the Tests against France, and went on to play in the 1968 World Cup down-under. It proved to be an unsuccessful tournament for Great Britain, who failed to qualify for the Final after losing to France. They were captained by Clark's Leeds team-mate Bev Risman, after Neil Fox (the original choice as captain) had to pull out with a leg injury.

Two of the game's greatest stars bade farewell in 1968 - Tom Van Vollenhoven who went home to South Africa from St.Helens, and Billy Boston who retired at Wigan. It was a popular complaint that the game was losing its stars, but the World Cup campaign produced a new one for the future in flying winger Clive Sullivan.

The fourth World Cup tournament was staged in 1968, in Australia with a couple of games in New Zealand (one of which did not actually feature the Kiwis as Great Britain lost to France at Auckland's Carlaw Park.) Australia won the World Cup, beating France 20-2 in the final at the Sydney Cricket Ground in front of a 54,290 Monday afternoon crowd. A star of the tournament for the Aussies was a 19-years-old winger from Queensland called John Rhodes *(pictured above on the attack against France in the final).*

The year of assissination and civil unrest in many parts of the world. Riots on the streets of Paris meant the French Rugby League team, on their way to Australia for the World Cup, got the last flight out before the airport was closed. Fans at home dreaded too much injury time as they might not get home in time to watch "The Monkees."

HITS HEARD ON THE TANNOY AT YOUR LOCAL R.L. GROUND
* *Hey Jude* - The Beatles
* *Born To Be Wild* - Steppenwolf
* *Dock of the Bay* - Otis Redding
* *Jumpin' Jack Flash* - Rolling Stones
* *Delilah* - Tom Jones

(Above) Yorkshire rivals Hunslet and Featherstone Rovers clash at the old Parkside ground, with Featherstone's Mike Smith within touching distance of the line. It was 1968 and Hunslet's glorious day at Wembley just three years earlier seemed like a distant memory. Featherstone were the Cup holders, but went out in the quarter-final in 1968 at Huddersfield, 9-7.

Leeds produce the expansive style coached by Roy Francis

When Leeds hammered Wigan 25-4 in the 1968 Challenge Cup semi-final at Swinton, it signalled a real changing of the guard in English Rugby League. Leeds, coached by Roy Francis, had become famous for their stylish and expansive attacking play, and to reach the game's biggest stage at Wembley for the first time since 1957 put the seal on Roy's work with the Loiners. As the Leeds backs, especially winger John Atkinson, dazzled their Wigan opponents on the hard ground at a sun-baked Station Road, it was a sad confirmation that some of the all-time greats, like Billy Boston and Eric Ashton, might be past their best. Atkinson is pictured *(above)* beating Wigan scrum-half Frankie Parr before scorching in for a try. Captained by front-rower Mick Clark, Leeds went

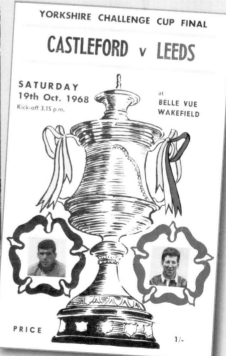

on to win at Wembley in the most sensational of circumstances against Wakefield. Much less controversial was a win over Castleford later in 1968 in the Yorkshire Cup Final.

1969

WINNERS:
Challenge Cup: Castleford.
Championship: Leeds.
Lancashire League: St.Helens.
Yorkshire League: Leeds.
Lancashire Cup: Swinton.
Yorkshire Cup: Hull.
County Championship: Lancashire.
Lance Todd Trophy: Malcolm Reilly (Castleford).

* Castleford win the Challenge Cup.
* Salford rekindle glories of the Red Devils.
* Leeds win a title and a European crown.
* Liverpool say goodbye, Huyton say hello.

(Above)
Hull F.C.'s Jim Macklin passes to Clive Sullivan in a 1969 derby. After a pretty lean decade throughout the 'sixties, Hull F.C. finally got their hands on a major trophy again when they won the Yorkshire Cup in 1969.

Castleford had become one of the game's top teams in the 'sixties as the nickname "Classy Cas" was invented and they, more than any other club, thrived on the publicity given by the game's growing presence on television. It had all begun in 1963-64 when ABC showed the junior games from Wheldon Road which made a schoolboy star of Roger Millward, and the arrival of the BBC Floodlit Trophy saw Castleford become the new Rugby League royalty, with Alan Hardisty and Keith Hepworth its crown princes. They had gone close before and become famous for the sparkling football created by that legendary half-back combination, but in 1969 Cas' finally achieved their dream of going to Wembley, where they won the Cup beating Salford 11-6. With "Rocky" Turner as their coach, Castleford had a hard edge to go with their attacking

(Above) **The 1969 Challenge Cup Final at Wembley and Castleford centre Keith Howe attempts to evade the Salford full-back Ken Gwilliam. Howe scored a try and Castleford finished on top to win 11-6 in front of a Wembley crowd of 97,939.**

Wembley sing-song

At the last Wembley Cup Final of the 'sixties, in 1969, these were the songs the crowd enjoyed, as printed on their community singing song-sheets:

1 - *"When you're smiling."*
2 - *"My girl's a Yorkshire girl."*
3 - *"She's a lassie from Lancashire."*
4 - *"Ob-la-di, ob-la-da."*
5 - *"Boom bang-a-bang."*
6 - *"Yellow submarine."*
7 - *"Puppet on a string."*
8 - *"Pack up your troubles in your old kit bag."*
9 - *"When the Saints go marching in."*
10 - *"For me and my gal."*
11 - *"John Brown's body."*

DAILY EXPRESS COMMUNITY SINGING

RUGBY LEAGUE CUP FINAL
CASTLEFORD
v
SALFORD
SATURDAY, 17 MAY 1969

Lancashire the 1969 County Champions

(Above) Alan Hardisty lifts the Challenge Cup for Castleford.

Lancashire became the final County Champions of the decade when they beat both Yorkshire and Cumberland to take the title in 1969. The Red Rose team *(above)* is pictured before playing Yorkshire at Salford on Wednesday, 3rd September 1969 - Lancashire winning 14-12. The players are, left to right: *(Back row):* John Stephens (Wigan), Billy Davies (Swinton), Geoff Fletcher (Wigan), Bob Welding (Leigh), George Nicholls (Widnes), Kevin Taylor (Oldham). *(Front row):* Parry Gordon (Warrington), Ray Dutton (Widnes), Chris Hesketh (Salford), Doug Laughton (Wigan) captain, Les Jones (St.Helens), Mike Murray (Barrow) and Billy Benyon (St.Helens).

skills, as the Red Devils discovered at Wembley. And no quarter was asked or given a week later when Cas' played Leeds in the Championship Final, seeking a double. The Loiners prevailed by two points to take their second Championship (the first was in 1961).

Salford's achievement in reaching Wembley for the first time since pre-War days, was a reward for all the investment by their chairman Brian Snape. The "Red Devils" were on the rise again and, although Wembley would elude them in the future, they became the most fashionable club in the game in the decade that followed. Leeds added to their Championship title by being crowned European Champions after a special match arranged against the French champions from Perpignan.

(Above) Bill Martin.

Meanwhile, away from the big clubs, a miraculous revival occurred at Whitehaven, a club who rose from near bankruptcy in the summer of 1969 to an unprecedented run of success under player-coach Sol Roper, which saw them top the League at one point. One of the major figures in this revival was the former Workington veteran, big Bill Martin, enjoying a real Indian Summer to his career. Those were happy times in the Autumn of 1969 as the 'sixties drew to a close.

IN 1969

Woodstock captured a few headlines in the world of popular music, but could not compare with Freddie and the Dreamers, who once had a show at a club in Leigh interrupted mid-song so an announcement could be made that Alex Murphy had just signed on at Hilton Park. This was the year when man first walked on the moon, Barrow signed Keith Jarrett and still the Rugby League clubs of England were arguing over a fixture format.

HITS HEARD ON THE TANNOY AT YOUR LOCAL R.L. GROUND
* *Pinball Wizard* - The Who
* *Proud Mary* - Creedence Clearwater Revival
* *Get Back* - The Beatles
* *My Cherie Amour* - Stevie Wonder
* *Marrakesh Express* - Crosby, Stills and Nash

Dud Beattie admits: "I goaded Turner!"

The 1962 Third Test in Sydney was one of the most sensational matches in Ashes history as Great Britain were denied a cleansweep series victory by one point after a highly controversial late try and touchline conversion by Ken Irvine. It became part of Ashes folklore when Great Britain's "Rocky" Turner was sent off after being provoked into a confrontation by an injured Aussie forward. This was how PETER MUSZKAT, one of the leading Australian reporters of the time, reflected on the incident.

(Above) **Turner shows his anger after being sent off alongside the injured Australian Dud Beattie.**

Dud Beattie, the Australian forward, admitted goading Derek Turner, the British vice-captain, into being sent off in the sensational third Test at the Sydney Cricket Ground.

Beattie, 28, had played through most of the first half in agony with displaced ribs. He later said he realised shortly after half-time that he could not stand the pain much longer. "So I decided to take an Englishman with me to even matters up," he admitted.

Beattie, who emerged from their Test triumph as Australia's unsung hero, set his sights on Turner. The English lock was in devastating form at the time. (In Brisbane last month, Turner was ordered off the field late in the clash with Queensland for kicking at Beattie. They had figured in several scuffles early in that match.)

Any trick is fair play in a Test. Englishmen have done more fooling than Australians in Test matches, and Beattie risked a severe pummelling from Turner just to help his team. "I knew I couldn't stand the pain any longer, when I went after Turner," Beattie said. "It is common knowledge that I was the aggressor."

Ian Walsh, Australia's Test hooker and vice-captain, "woke"

to Beattie's courageous tactics as soon as he saw the fight erupt after 12 minutes of the second half. "I knew straight away what Dud was up to," Walsh said. "He did Australia a big service by removing a fully fit Englishman from the game, while Dud himself could hardly stand up.

"He was in terrific pain and could not pack down into the front-row because the weight was killing him. Dud spent most of the game in the second-row. At one stage, when we lost a few scrums in a row, I asked him to come back into the front-row but he said he couldn't do it."

Walsh said that Beattie at no stage was given instuctions to take Turner or any other English forward off the field with him. "Dud did it all off his own bat and we were all very proud of him," the Australian vice-captain said.

Beattie's successful move has incensed the British team. Turner declined to comment on Beattie or the incident. All members of the British team are forbidden by contract to make press comments. But in a report today, Mr. Stuart Hadfield, the British manager, accused Australia of having acted unsportingly over the Beattie-Turner incident."

(Adapted from Peter Muszkat's report in the Sydney 'Daily Mirror' on 17th July, 1962.)

KANGAROOS AT WILDERSPOOL

Photos by EDDIE WHITHAM

Official RUGBY LEAGUE Year Book 1962

E.E. Christensen's

Noel Kelly, Billy Smith and Johnny Raper are some of the biggest names in Australian Rugby League featured in these pictures from the 1967 Kangaroo tour opening match versus Warrington at Wilderspool.

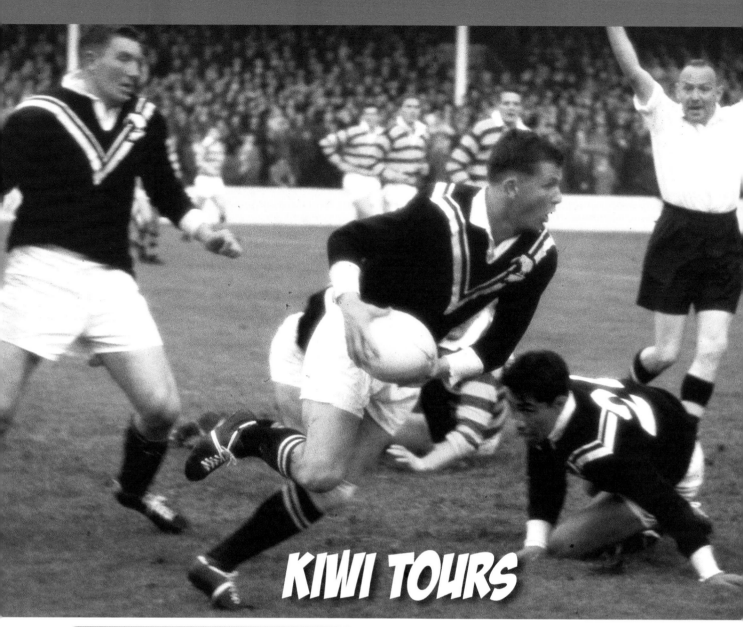

KIWI TOURS

1961 KIWI TOUR IN ENGLAND

Widnes-Liverpool	lost	6-9	9,050
Manchester XIII-Swinton-Salford	lost	7-19	6,926
Castleford-Featherstone	won	31-20	5,744
Leeds City XIII	won	24-9	7,085
Oldham-Rochdale H.	lost	8-10	8,795
Yorkshire (Hull K.R)	lost	11-21	6,750
Barrow	won	36-11	6,647
Lancashire (Warrington)	lost	13-15	9,332
Huddersfield-Halifax	won	31-11	7,251
Rugby League XIII (Manchester)	lost	20-22	5,271
Warrington	won	21-9	8,959
GT.BRITAIN (Leeds)	**won**	**29-11**	**16,540**
Hull-Hull K.R.	lost	6-17	8,125
Wigan	lost	6-28	25,483
Whitehaven-Workington	won	10-9	4,970
St. Helens	lost	10-25	21,680
GT.BRITAIN (Bradford)	**lost**	**10-23**	**19,980**
Leigh	won	15-4	6,584
Wakefield T.	lost	7-20	16,558
GT.BRITAIN (Swinton)	**lost**	**19-35**	**22,536**

(Above) **The 1965 New Zealand touring team in action versus Warrington at Wilderspool, with Dennis Davies the referee. The Kiwis won this fixture 14-7.**

One of the great romantic adventures of international Rugby League was the amateurs of New Zealand going on tour to Europe and taking on the best players of England and France. The Kiwis' two European tours of the 'sixties, both in 1961 and 1965, were not too successful on the field in terms of wins and losses, but left enduring memories of fine football and excellent sportsmen. The 1961 team, captained by Don Hammond, gave Great Britain an almighty shock in the first Test at Headingley, and were a young side of talented players who went on to represent New Zealand well throughout the rest of the

(Left)
The 1965 Kiwi touring team pictured outside their hotel in Ilkley - the traditional base for Rugby League touring sides whilst in the north of England. The New Zealanders were captained by half-back Bill Snowden and didn't win a Test in England.

decade. Several returned in 1965 and went on to establish themselves as legends of New Zealand Rugby League - not least the centre Roger Bailey (the 'baby' of the team in 1961), half-back Bill Snowden (who captained the Kiwis on the 1965 tour), Don Hammond himself, and the two formidable Maori props Maunga Emery and Sam Edwards. Both Kiwi tours broke interesting new ground for the game in England, with the 1961 team playing a "Rugby League X111" under floodlights at Manchester's White City stadium - a crowd of 5,271 turned out to see an entertaining match won 22-20 by the "home" side made up largely of overseas stars and ex-Rugby Union men, given a rare chance to win representative honours in Rugby League. The format was repeated when the 1965 Kiwis played a "Commonwealth X111" at London's Crystal Palace. Attendances had begun to fall in English Rugby League by the time the 1965 Kiwis arrived, and the New Zealanders failed to ignite too much excitement among British fans resulting in very poor crowds for two of the three Test matches.

(Above) Great Britain loose-forward Roy Evans touches down versus the 1961 Kiwis.

1965 KIWI TOUR IN ENGLAND

Commonwealth XIII (Crystal Pal.)	won	15-7	1,200
Bradford N.	lost	15-28	8,373
Warrington	won	14-7	8,162
Halifax	won	24-12	6,730
Oldham	won	5-2	13,021
Wigan	won	17-12	12,853
Widnes	lost	3-8	9,450
Hull K.R.	won	21-11	7,540
St. Helens	lost	7-28	11,270
Leeds	won	28-13	5,782
Yorkshire (Castleford)	lost	8-15	14,814
GT.BRITAIN (Swinton)	**lost**	**2-7**	**8,541**
Leigh	won	10-5	4,840
Barrow	won	20-10	5,081
Whitehaven	lost	7-12	3,208
Castleford	won	7-6	5,702
Hull	won	11-8	6,591
Lancashire (St. Helens)	won	21-10	8,781
Rochdale H.	won	10-4	7,075
GT.BRITAIN (Bradford)	**lost**	**9-15**	**15,740**
Swinton	lost	7-14	8,345
Wakefield T.	lost	4-16	7,484
GT.BRITAIN (Wigan)	**drew**	**9-9**	**7,919**

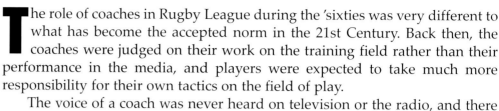

The role of coaches in Rugby League during the 'sixties was very different to what has become the accepted norm in the 21st Century. Back then, the coaches were judged on their work on the training field rather than their performance in the media, and players were expected to take much more responsibility for their own tactics on the field of play.

The voice of a coach was never heard on television or the radio, and there were no after-match quotes dominating newspaper reports. Whilst every club wanted a capable figurehead to train and guide their team, the importance of the "coach" did not rank very highly in the view of the game's authorities when it came to international Rugby League. Throughout the 'sixties the Australians were happy to have the captain of their team also take on the coaching mantle, whilst Great Britain paid little heed to appointing a coach and for much of the decade were happy to let the R.F.L. secretary Bill Fallowfield don his tracksuit and oversee training sessions before international matches, including the successful 1960 World Cup.

However, despite not being given the media profile of the modern day coach, there were some very influentual figures who shaped the game in the 'sixties, not least the duo of Colin Hutton and Roy Francis who were at the cutting edge of Rugby League throughout the decade.

Colin Hutton did it all at both club and international levels. He was the man who took Hull K.R. from

(Above)
Colin Hutton as Great Britain coach in 1968.

(Above) **Roy Francis - a coach ahead of his time in the 1960s.**

being perennial basement dwellers to becoming one of the league's top teams in the 1960s. Colin was at the helm for the Robins throughout the 'sixties as they regularly challenged for the top honours - going to Wembley, playing in a Championship Final and winning the Yorkshire Cup - he was also a major figure in the Rugby League's Coaching Scheme. In the international arena Colin Hutton was there with one of Great Britain's best ever teams in Australia, the 1962 Lions, although the R.F.L. did not bestow the title of "coach" on him following the problems which had arisen on the previous tour. Instead, Colin was described as the "trainer and baggage man" as Great Britain retained the Ashes in sensational style. He returned to Australia for a second tour in 1968 with the World Cup team.

Roy Francis had been Hutton's club coach at Hull during their glory days of the 1950s, and was often described as being a man many years ahead of his time with his more scientific approach to training and preparation for matches. Roy moved to Leeds in 1963

(Above)
Joe Coan greets his Saints captain Alex Murphy after victory at Wembley in 1966.

and built a successful team renowned for its entertaining style - his reputation was so high that he was recruited by the North Sydney club in 1969 on a three-year 30,000 dollar contract which, according to many good judges, made him Australian Rugby League's first so-called "master coach." Not only was Roy Francis a trained physiotherapist he was also a pioneer of sports psychology.

Griff Jenkins was, like Roy Francis, a Welshman (albeit born in Warrington) who was a dominant figure in coaching after establishing his reputation as the helm of the great Oldham team of the 1950s. Griff had a spell with Halifax in the early 'sixties before being head-hunted by Wigan, who remembered all too well the dominance his Oldham sides had held over them just a few years earlier. Jenkins took Wigan to Wembley in 1963 before he left Central Park, then in May 1964 he became secretary-coach of Salford as the first major appointment made by their new chairman Brian Snape. For the next six years, throughout the 'sixties, Griff Jenkins was in charge of the Red Devils as they rose from the lower ranks to become the glamour team of the game. His time with Salford climaxed with guiding them to Wembley in 1969.

The third member of the Welsh trio of "master coaches" in the 'sixties was **Cliff Evans,** the supremo behind Swinton's famous back-to-back Championship titles in 1963 and 1964. By the end of the decade Cliff had been recruited by St.Helens, and his glory came with them when he coached Saints to the Championship in 1969-70. Later in 1970, he succeeded Griff Jenkins at Salford and guided the Red Devils into their Championship winning years of the mid 'seventies.

(Above)
Left to right:
Cliff Evans, Ken Traill, Joe Warham and Albert Fearnley. Four of the major successful figures in coaching and football management during the 1960s in British Rugby League. All brought major trophies to their clubs (Swinton, Wakefield Trinity, Leeds and Halifax respectively.)

One essential ingredient needed to be a successful coach, in addition to being able to man-manage the players, was to have a good knowledge of physical fitness training. And St.Helens took this to a new extreme when they appointed **Joe Coan** as their coach in the 1965-66 season. Joe hailed from Whitehaven and worked as a P.T. teacher in St.Helens, and had no background experience at all in Rugby League - never having played the game or coached it even at junior level. But he stepped straight into the hot seat at Knowsley Road and, despite being little older than several of the players, he created a highly successful combination which won the league and cup double and went within a whisker of winning 'All Four Cups.' Coan enjoyed a successful few years at St.Helens, and was later recruited by Wigan. Saints players of the time had great respect for his organisational abilities and his intelligence, whilst Joe himself admitted he left most of the footballing tactics to the players on the field.

Another two key figures in the evolvement of coaching in the 1960s were **Joe Warham** and **Albert Fearnley.** Joe was a dominant figure at Headingley, overseeing the recruitment and development of all the great Leeds sides of the decade, whilst Albert coached Halifax to the Championship title in 1965 before moving on to play a key role in the future successes of the reformed Bradford Northern and, with **Laurie Gant**, working on the National Coaching Scheme.

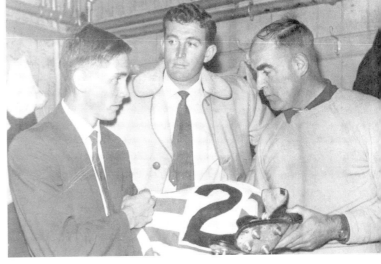

(Above)
Griff Jenkins, as the Wigan coach in 1962-3, welcomes two new signings from Rhodesia, Trevor Lake and John Winton, and gets them kitted out in the Central Park dressing-room.

Lions 1962 - truly great Britain

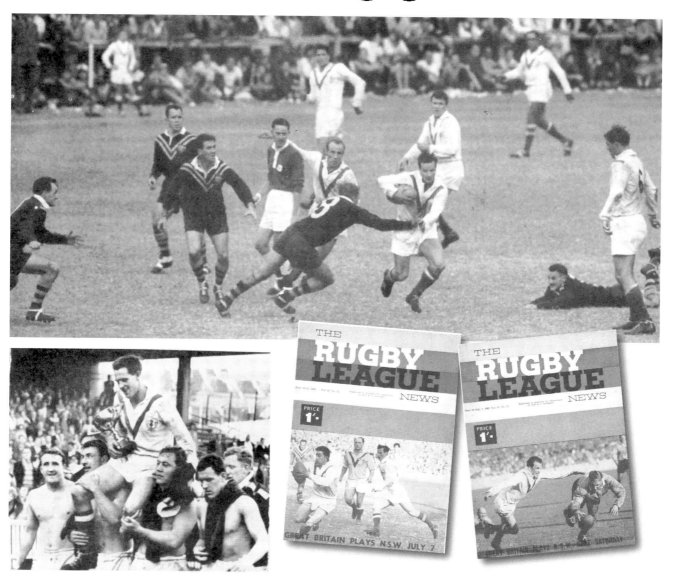

(Above)
Great Britain's captain Eric Ashton holds the Ashes trophy as he is carried on a lap of honour around the Sydney Cricket Ground in 1962.

(Top picture)
Alex Murphy skips through Australia's defence in Brisbane as the Ashes were won in the second Test of the 1962 series. Other British players are Harold Poynton, Neil Fox, Eric Ashton, Billy Boston and Brian Edgar.

Great Britain played eight Test matches in 1962, winning just two and losing six (those defeats came three against France, two by New Zealand and one by Australia.) Hardly the most impressive record, yet the British side of 1962 is remembered as one of our best ever - and certainly Australians believe it was the finest they ever saw on their shores. In winning the first two Tests of the Ashes series in Australia, the Great Britain team of 1962 conclusively brushed aside the Aussie challenge and were only denied a clean sweep in highly controversial circumstances in the third Test.

The 1962 Lions tour broke all records at the box-office, starting with an impressive crowd of 57,142 to see their first "big" match against Sydney. As a comparison between the two codes at that time, on the same day a Rugby Union Test match in Brisbane between Australia and the New Zealand All Blacks had a crowd of less than 12,000. The Lions backed up their 21-13 win over the Sydney side by returning to the Cricket Ground the following Saturday to beat the New South Wales state team in front of over 60,000, and when the first Test took place there seven days later, an all ticket crowd of 69,990 paid a new Australian record with receipts of £30,000. They saw a swashbuckling win by 31 points to 12 by a British side inspired by a magnificent performance by second-rower Dick Huddart.

(*Above*) **The Lions line up alongside the St.George team on the Sydney Cricket Ground before their famous Wednesday afternoon clash on the 1962 tour, when a crowd of 58,000 turned out to see the tourists thrash the local club champions.**

Captained by centre Eric Ashton, Great Britain clinched the Ashes by winning the second Test in Brisbane 17-10. The seven-point margin actually flattered the Australians, who were again outclassed by the brilliant forward play of McTigue, Huddart and Edgar, and despite the Lions having to play the last 25 minutes with 12 men after scrum-half Alex Murphy was carried off with a leg injury. Billy Boston scored two tries in the victory. This was the first Ashes Test match ever to be played at Brisbane's Lang Park, a ground that would grow to become Queensland's iconic venue.

Ashton's 1962 Lions were denied the glory of becoming the first ever British side to win all three Ashes Tests on Australian soil in the closing minutes of a highly charged third Test in Sydney. Despite playing with eleven men for much of the game after Mick Sullivan and Derek Turner had been sent off by referee D'Arcy Lawler, Great Britain were still leading 17-13 with just a couple of minutes left on the clock. Then Aussie winger Ken Irvine scored a try in the corner off a pass that was several yards forward, and proceeded to kick a magnificent conversion from the touchline, to give Australia an 18-17 win. Four days later, the British took some revenge by thrashing the champion club St.George in a match most Aussies predicted would be like a fourth Test. The Lions' exhibition of brilliant football put the seal on a superb tour to Australia.

(*Above*)
Mr. Stuart Hadfield as manager of the 1962 Great Britain touring team in Australia. Mr. Hadfield was also the Chairman of the Wakefield Trinity club during their Cup winning years of the early 'sixties.

(*Left*)
The British team at training in Sydney on the 1962 Lions tour. Leading the way are prop Norman Herbert and full-back Gary Cooper, followed by: Brian Edgar, John Taylor, Mick Sullivan, Alex Murphy, Eric Ashton, Billy Boston and Brian McTigue. No branded training gear was supplied in those days.

Great Britain Tests with France

(Above)
The British team at Perpignan in December 1962, before going on to lose 17-12 to France in a typically brutal and controversial encounter. Left to right: *(Standing):* **Laurie Gilfedder, Ken Bowman, Bill Martin, Mick Sullivan, Bill Drake, Ken Gowers, Derek Turner.** *(In front):* **Peter Flanagan, Tommy Smales, Eric Ashton (captain), Frank Myler, Bill Burgess and Neil Fox.**

The ability to play tough Test matches against France was a constant throughout the 'sixties for British Rugby League. Anglo-French internationals were not dismissed as mere preparation for Great Britain's future Tests against Australia and New Zealand, they were full blooded (often literally!) encounters which gave a focus to every season as discussion and speculation grew in the media about team selection and the national press correspondents covered the Test matches themselves in great detail.

The reporters certainly got no shortage of headlines from those Tests, especially the ones played on French soil, as controversy went hand in glove with these games between nations divided by language and from two very different cultures when it came to Rugby League. Matches between Great Britain and France had not been granted full Test status until 1957, and the 'sixties was the time when the cross-channel rivalry became most intense. Of twenty Tests played in the decade, the British won ten, the French nine, with one drawn.

Inevitably, the British complained about French referees, and often put their defeats in France down to "home bias" from the match officials. Equally, the French found it just as hard to accept the attitudes of some English referees, never more than in an infamous drama at Swinton in January 1965 when play was held up for over seven minutes after France's captain Marcel Bescos had been sent off by referee D. T. H. Davies but refused to leave the field, provoking a "walk off" by his team. Schoolmaster Davies had dismissed Bescos for persistent foul play and rule breaking, whereas the French thought he was getting his marching orders "merely for being offside." It was a classic case of the misunderstanding caused by the language barrier, but the unsavoury soap opera was played out in front of millions watching live on BBC television.

(Left) Great Britain line up before their Test at the Toulouse stadium in 1969. *(Below)* Britain's first Test at Carcassonne in 1967 and forwards Brian Tyson and Terry Fogerty face up to a strong French forager.

Much more attractive television viewing came 12 months later when the BBC, via the Eurovision link, broadcast live coverage from Perpignan of Great Britain's Test in France. There were no complaints about the refereeing on this occasion as the tough English official "Sergeant Major" Eric Clay took control, the French winning 18-13.

Whilst the Tests against France were littered with accusations of foul play and temperamental behaviour by the French, Great Britain only found them easy opponents when they travelled to the north of England for midweek games with severely weakened teams in 1963 and '64, losing heavily at Wigan and Leigh respectively (the latter under floodlights). Britain's finest moments against France came with home and away "doubles" in 1960-61, in the aftermath of winning the World Cup; and again in 1963-64 when, led by Tommy Smales, they recovered from losing the Ashes at home to Australia for the first time.

France's best "double" was in 1962, when they shocked a British side which went on to win the Ashes in Australia and be regarded as one of our best ever. The French won 20-15 in brilliant style at Wigan after overturning a 13-2 deficit. And they clinched the double back in Perpignan a month later. The two European nations also met in the decade's two World Cups, Great Britain winning at Swinton 33-7 in 1960, and losing 7-2 at Auckland's Carlaw Park in 1968.

ODSAL STADIUM - BRADFORD
RUGBY LEAGUE INTERNATIONAL MATCH
GREAT BRITAIN
versus
FRANCE
SATURDAY 2nd MARCH 1968
KICK-OFF 3-0 p.m
GRANDSTAND SECTION C
ROW E   SEAT NO. 17
15/-   G. W. Turton, Secretary
See Back for Plan of Entrance

1960s TEST RESULTS

1960 - 6th March *(at Toulouse)*
France 20, Great Britain 18.
1960 - 26th March *(at St.Helens)*
Great Britain 17, France 17.
1960 - 11th December *(at Bordeaux)*
France 10, Great Britain 21.
1961 - 28th January *(at St.Helens)*
Great Britain 27, France 8.
1962 - 17th February *(at Wigan)*
Great Britain 15, France 20.
1962 - 11th March *(at Perpignan)*
France 23, Great Britain 13.
1962 - 2nd December *(at Perpignan)*
France 17, Great Britain 12.
1963 - 3rd April *(at Wigan)*
Great Britain 42, France 4.
1964 - 8th March *(at Perpignan)*
France 5, Great Britain 11.
1964 - 18th March *(at Leigh)*
Great Britain 39, France 0.

1964 - 6th December *(at Perpignan)*
France 18, Great Britain 8.
1965 - 23rd January *(at Swinton)*
Great Britain 17, France 7.
1966 - 16th January *(at Perpignan)*
France 18, Great Britain 13.
1966 - 5th March *(at Wigan)*
Great Britain 4, France 8.
1967 - 22nd January *(at Carcassonne)*
France 13, Great Britain 16.
1967 - 4th March *(at Wigan)*
Great Britain 13, France 23.
1968 - 11th February *(at Paris)*
France 13, Great Britain 22.
1968 - 2nd March *(at Bradford)*
Great Britain 19, France 8.
1968 - 30th November *(at St.Helens)*
Great Britain 34, France 10.
1969 - 2nd February *(at Toulouse)*
France 13, Great Britain 9.

Totals: **Played 20; Great Britain won 10; France won 9; drawn one.**

Bill Fallowfield: "I don't seek popularity"

Bill Fallowfield, dominated Rugby League in Britain throughout the 'sixties, and he regularly called for rule changes that would put an end to teams being able to dominate possession of the ball. Finally, Bill got his way with the introduction of the four tackle rule in 1966, but that didn't end his quest to change the rules even more. Rarely did Bill Fallowfield make public his personal thoughts on being un-popular or being labelled a dictator by many. This interview with Bill was published in Australia shortly after the 1968 World Cup tournament.

(Above) **Bill Fallowfield in 1968 as Great Britain's manager at the World Cup in Australia - the time this interview with Bill was first published.**

Bill Fallowfield says: "If I live to see the play-the-ball scrapped I'll be a happy man." Heresy! But it's the sort of thing that Bill Fallowfield tosses casually into the ring a dozen times a day. Aha, you say. That explains it. It's that Fallowfield again. Fallowfield the dictator!

Yes, it was that man Fallowfield again but whether you regard him as a dictator or not is a matter of opinion. And whatever you regard him as it's not likely to make the slightest difference to Bill Fallowfield. He's been called a dictator, des-pot, Mr. English Rugby League, strongman, big boss, autocrat .... you name it, Fallowfield's been called it.

Think up a new cliche to tag him and he'll probably thank you for a touch of originality. Then he will tell you just as firmly: "It really is time we scrapped the play-the-ball rule." It may sound like heresy, it may sound like madness, but when Bill Fallowfield suggests a rule change it's time to sit up and take notice.

Fallowfield's last rule-juggling brainchild was the four-tackle rule. Since it was introduced in England, Rugby League, which had gone into a slow decline, has started to pick up attendances for the first time in nearly two decades. In France, where the speed and variety needed for the four-tackle rule suits the local temperament, the game is rushing back to the peak in popularity it enjoyed in the Puig-Aubert era. Australia has never experienced football fever quite like that of the past two seasons since the new rule came into force. On that basis alone, anything Fallowfield says about rule-changing deserves to be listened to:

"Changing the play-the-ball rule is the next logical development," he says. "The obvious step is to cut out all the rules relating to heeling the ball. If there are no rules there can be no prob-lems. The play-the-ball is merely a way of getting the ball back into play. These days the opposing player never strikes for the ball because that means the referee must start the four-tackle count all over again.

"Yet we still have a mass of technical rules governing how we should play the ball, with dif-ferent interpretations in different countries. The result is dozens of penalties which slow up the game and serve no useful purpose. If we elimi-nate those rules we would also eliminate the penalties.

"The purpose of the four-tackle rule is to give one side the ball four times in succession. Why not have the tackled player just put the ball on the ground and heel it back - no rules, no penalties, no problems."

It's hard to find fault with the logic of Mr. Fallowfield's argument, yet when he finally gets around to proposing its introduction it is sure to be greeted with a scream of rage. That Fallowfield is tinkering with the rules again, the diehards will say. But the charge is not likely to turn one steel-grey hair on Bill Fallowfield's balding head.

"Whenever one tries to change the game he is accused of tinkering," Fallowfield says. "Tinkering, to my mind, is reverting to something that has been tried and found wanting. Someone is always plugging for the one-yard or three-yard or five-yard rules, when all have been tried."

But Bill Fallowfield is prepared for the shock, the outrage, the abuse. He has become used to it since he first became secretary of the English Rugby League in 1946. As architect of the four-tackle rule he copped enough for his corner when the rule was first used in England two years ago. But he has lived to see most of his critics grudgingly accept the rule as a vast improvement.

"The new rule has converted the game into a fast entertaining spectacle," he says. "In the past this was possible only when both sides were prepared to throw the ball about. Now they *have* to throw it about. Possession is no longer the be all and end all of the game. I remember one English captain telling his team: *'Let's keep the ball, they can't score if we have it.'* "

Mr. Fallowfield is convinced we have yet to see the best of the four-tackle rule. He says the rule will not be used to its greatest effect until the new breed of footballer now growing up with the rule reaches the top grades.

"Many of the present-day players, even the internationals, are living in the past," he says. "They are still thinking of possession all the time when they should be thinking of varying the attack. They still have not eradicated their bad habits of the past. They have not yet realised that when they say goodbye to the ball it's not goodbye forever."

Fallowfield pointed to the Great Britain v. France World Cup match in Auckland this year as an example of the inability of some top English players to adapt to new conditions.

"That was a game in which we should have been kicking all the time," he says. "In that mudbath it was no day for handling. The Frenchmen kept kicking and they won. The top players, brought up under the old rules, still have not learnt to use their feet skilfully enough. I know some internationals who not only won't kick the ball - they can't kick it."

(Above) **Bill Fallowfield, in tracksuit, demonstrates how to pass the ball at a coaching course in the early 1960s.**

Fallowfield would like to see teams develop in which every player, forward and back, can use his feet to introduce variety into the attack. He wants to see the cross-kick to the wing, grubber-kick and up-and-under used constantly to speed up play. The result, he says, will be Rugby League such as has never been seen before.

"Just one good tactical kicker can make a vast difference to a team," he says.

The faster, more spectacular brand of football is not the only benefit from the four tackle rule, according to its creator.

"The rule has cut foul play down dramatically," says Fallowfield. "The number of players dismissed from the field last season in England was much lower than in the previous two or three seasons. There is not so much barging in the game now. The forwards are trying to avoid being tackled. There is less bodily contact and so there is less friction."

But the man who fathered the four tackle rule is not ging to sit back now. He wants to see more rule changes - not as revolutionary as the four tackle rule, perhaps, but smaller changes that will cut down on the number of penalities. Elimination of the technicalities in the play-the-ball for instance, and revision of the scrummaging rules.

When Mr. Fallowfield finally proposes his rule changes to the International Board, he is sure to come under fire from many quarters. There are those who will resort to the familiar cry that Fallowfield is a dictator. They are no more likely to upset him than they ever have.

"I speak my mind and I suppose that's one good way to get enemies," he says. "If I get my own way I'm called a dictator. But the truth is that the Rugby League Council, not me, is the governing body for the game in England. The council often does things that I don't personally agree with and I get the blame.

"Of course, the council also often accepts my ideas and advice. This is natural enough - I'm a fulltime secretary but the chairman changes every year. This throws a lot of responsibility on my shoulders, particularly at international level.

"I've been given certain powers and I'm not afraid to use them. Personally, I'd like to be popular, but I don't go about seeking popularity."

DOWN TO SWINGING LONDON

(Pictured)
An illustration of how Rugby League could attract the highest profile guests to big matches staged in London as (above, right) Prime Minister Harold Wilson meets the Australian team before the White City Test match in 1967, and (far right) Prince Philip, the Duke of Edinburgh, is introduced by Great Britain captain Eric Ashton to his players before the Wembley 1963 Ashes opener.

London had not had its own professional Rugby League club since the 1930s, and would not have one again until Fulham came on the scene in 1980, yet throughout the 'sixties the game was no stranger to the capital city in addition to the annual pilgrammage to the Cup Final at Wembley.

Both the Ashes series staged on British soil during the 'sixties included a Test match played in London, which was an illustration of the adventurous spirit of the Rugby Football League in those days despite the restrictions in transport links and far smaller access to private cars. That willingness to push back new frontieers was further illustrated by the fact that both those London Test matches, in 1963 and 1967, were night games played under floodlights.

The League's sense of adventure did prove to be a fairly costly risk for the first of those Tests, in 1963 at Wembley, when an attendance of only 14,000 turned up for a match that would have drawn at least 30,000 in the north of England. Had that first Test been staged on the usual Saturday afternoon there was every chance that thousands more Rugby League fans from the north would have travelled to Wembley, but on a Wednesday night with work and school the next morning that was a fairly forlorn hope. Torrential rain on the night would not have helped encourage a "walk up" audience, but it was obvious that the vast majority of those 14,000 spectators at Wembley on 16th October 1963 were locally based in London and the south-east, with few travelling from the Rugby League heartlands of the north.

Four years later, when the 1967 Kangaroos came on tour to the U.K., the Australians again expressed their desire to play one of the Tests in London, and this time the White City in Shepherds Bush was chosen as the venue for the second Test in the Ashes series. Again the match was played under floodlights, but at least this one was on a Friday night rather than midweek, and the west London location of the White City made it much more amenable to the capital's Australian residents.

THE RUGBY FOOTBALL LEAGUE

FIRST TEST MATCH
GREAT BRITAIN
v
AUSTRALIA

WEDNESDAY, OCTOBER 16th   KICK-OFF 7.30 p.m.

WEMBLEY
EMPIRE STADIUM

OFFICIAL PROGRAMME · · · ONE SHILLING

As early as April of that year, the R.F.L.'s publicity was urging fans to make a note of the date, 3rd November 1967: "because it provides you with an excuse for another weekend in *'swinging London.'"* Seating tickets for the Test match at the White City stadium in Wood Lane, Shepherds Bush, London W.12., were available in advance priced £1, 15 shillings and 10 shillings, with some restaurant tickets available at £2. Those supporters who travelled from the north, took a stroll down Carnaby Street and then headed out to the White City, were joined by a large contingent of Australians in a vibrant crowd of 17,445, which probably exceeded expectations at the time.

(Above)
Action from the 1967 Test match at the White City, which Australia won to level the series. British players in the picture include Ian Brooke, Frank Foster and Peter Flanagan. It proved to be Foster's only Test match appearance.

Staging an Ashes Test match at the White City in 1967 was not done in isolation because Rugby League activity in London had been gathering pace for a while before then. In 1965, on a Thursday night in August, Rugby League participated in a Festival of Sport at Crystal Palace with a seven-a-side tournament involving several of the game's top professional clubs. Most of the leading clubs expressed a desire to take part in this London tournament which, in the event, was won by Wigan who beat Workington Town 14-13 in the final.

(Left)
Wembley 1963 saw injury-hit Great Britain suffer a big defeat to the Aussies in heavy rain. In this picture, centre Neil Fox is well covered by the Kangaroos' defence, led by hooker Ian Walsh.

Six days later, on Wednesday 18th August 1965, Rugby League returned to Crystal Palace when the New Zealanders opened their tour with a fixture against a 'Commonwealth X111' - the Kiwis won 15-7, before a crowd reported as "less than 2,000." The positive result from these two events at Crystal Palace was the revival of the amateur game in London with the formation of the Southern Amateur Rugby League. Their principal organiser was secretary Tom Clarke, and soon teams including Ealing, Hillingdon, Peckham and Hackney were taking part in regular Sunday morning games, with another notable side travelling from Portsmouth.

The R.F.L. provided regular publicity for the amateurs' annual dance held at the Railway Hotel in Greenford, Middlesex, on the eve of the Challenge Cup Final, and the league's progress continued to the point that by the end of the 'sixties, in 1969, the Southern Amateur Rugby League Sevens tournament was contested by a record 14 teams. The winners were the powerful Parachute Regiment side from Aldershot who received the trophy from the league's chairman Vic Peacock - the cup had been kindly donated by Keith Macklin, the well known journalist and broadcaster. Another media personality, the BBC commentator Eddie Waring, also became a great supporter of the Southern Amateur League, and agreed to become its honorary president.

THE RUGBY FOOTBALL LEAGUE

GREAT BRITAIN

v.

AUSTRALIA

TEST MATCH
at WHITE CITY, LONDON
FRIDAY, 3rd NOVEMBER, 1967
KICK-OFF 7.45 p.m.
OFFICIAL PROGRAMME
ONE SHILLING

Wales – the forgotten decade

(Above)
Wales in action versus England at Leeds on 18th October 1969. The Welsh props Jim Mills and Graham Rees are pictured bringing the English full-back Arthur Keegan to ground, as centre Peter Rowe lends a hand with the defensive duties. Other Welsh players in the background are Bob Prosser and John Mantle, whilst the Englishmen include Roger Millward, Chris Hesketh and Johnny Ward. Wales were beaten 40-23 in this high-scoring game at Headingley in the European Championship.

Despite the presence of a hatful of outstanding Welsh players in Rugby League throughout the 'Sixties, it was very much a forgotten decade for the game in Wales with not a single international match being staged in the Principality. No Welsh national team took the field for a fully recognised international match in the 'sixties until November 1968 - although the red jerseys were worn with just as much pride when a "Welsh X111" travelled to Toulouse to play France in February 1963.

The decade began with three of Rugby League's all-time greats in full flow, all of them Welshmen: Billy Boston, Lewis Jones and Tommy Harris - indeed, both Boston and Harris were in Great Britain's World Cup winning squad of 1960. And a steady stream of Welsh recruits continued to "go north" to cash in on their talents in the professional ranks which, with hindsight, seems to make a mockery of the belief at the time that there were not enough quality players available to provide the strength in depth to put together a consistently competitive Wales team.

There were dozens of top class Welsh Rugby League players around in the 1960s, but the problem seemed to be filling the specialist role of hooker - so vital in those days when winning possession from the scrums was a key skill, and especially important in the years before the four-tackle rule was introduced in 1966. After Tommy Harris retired in the early part of the decade, Wales had no recognised hooker until Tony Fisher came on the scene in the late 'sixties. It may be purely coincidental, but as soon as Fisher was established with Bradford Northern, that's when it was deemed possible to re-launch a Welsh team.

The motivation for the revival of Wales in international Rugby League, which came in the 1968-69 season, had much more to do with the public interest created by the signing of Welsh Rugby Union "golden boys" David Watkins and Terry Price (by Salford and Bradford Northern respectively) followed by

Keith Jarrett (to Barrow) soon after. That, and the continued desire of the French Rugby League to have an annual international tournament, finally saw a Welsh team back on the field, but it only lasted for two seasons and they never got to play on home soil.

The first sighting of a Welsh team in the 'sixties came when they played in France in the 1962-63 season. Captained by Lewis Jones, the players struggled for fitness in the warm Toulouse sunshine having come from the "big freeze" in the U.K. which had left them inactive for many weeks. They lost 23-3 with their only points coming from Ray Glastonbury, the Workington Town winger who was on his way to becoming the game's top try-scorer in his debut season in Rugby League.

After another gap of six years, the revival of the Welsh team came on a Thursday night at Salford in November 1968, when they took on England and beat them 24-17. This was a Welsh side including a new generation of stars like Clive Sullivan, David Watkins, Bob Prosser, John Warlow, John Mantle and Kel Coslett. They returned to action later that season in March 1969, going down 17-13 to France at the *Parc des Princes* in Paris. The strength of the Welsh team prompted a fully fledged revival of the European Championship in 1969-70, and their last games of the decade saw Wales lose 40-23 to England at Headingley in October 1969 before suf-

(Above)
Dennis Brown, the Widnes winger, on the attack for Wales as they met France at the Parc des Princes in Paris in March 1969.

(Below)
Kel Coslett in action in that same match at Parc des Princes in which the Welsh team played extremely well and were unlucky to lose by 17-13 to a strong French side. St.Helens star Coslett played second-row for Wales, having been at full-back in the 1963 Welsh X111 in France.

(Above) **The Welsh X111 before playing France at the Toulouse Stadium in February 1963. Left to right: *(Standing)*: Charlie Winslade, Idwal Fisher, Colin Dixon, Terry Robbins, Johnny Freeman, Ron Morgan, Stan Owen, Kel Coslett. *(In front)*: Gordon Lewis, Lewis Jone (captain), Colin Evans, Ray Glastonbury and Don Vines. This Welsh side was beaten 23-3.**

fering another defeat, 8-2 to France, at Salford five days later.

So, a total record in the 'sixties of: Played only five matches; won one and lost four, was a poor return for Wales in a decade when so many talented Welsh players were in Rugby League. Just look at some of these names of Welshman in the game then (and this is by no means a list of every player available in the 1960s): *Full-backs:* Garfield Owen, Ronnie James, Terry Price, Keith Jarrett; *Wingers:* Billy Boston, Johnny Freeman, Clive Sullivan, Ray Glastonbury, Frank Wilson, Dennis Brown, Keri Jones, Terry O'Brien, Maurice Richards. *Centres:* Malcolm Price, Gordon Lewis, Peter Rowe, David Jones, Alex Kersey-Brown; *Half-backs:* Lewis Jones, Alan Rees, David Watkins, Colin Evans, Bob Prosser, Phil Morgan. *Forwards:* Stan Owen, Graham Rees, Charlie Winslade, Ron Morgan, Don Vines, Jim Mills, John Warlow, Tommy Harris, Colin Dixon, Mervyn Hicks, John Mantle, Tony Fisher, Bobby Wanbon, Kel Coslett, Ron Hill ... several were Great Britain Test players and would have done Wales proud.

(Above) Great Britain Under-24s at Bayonne in France on 26th November 1966. Left to right: *(Standing):* Ian Hare, Alan McGlone, Bill Pattinson, Bob Haigh, Mick Harrison, Bob Irving, John Stephens, Barry Simpson. *(In front):* Clive Sullivan, Parry Gordon, Colin Tyrer, Alan Burwell (capt.), Tommy Warburton, Chris Hesketh and Jack Gamble.

(Above)
Proof that the British boys really did have to wear a French club kit in their very first Under-24 interntional match, played in Toulouse in April 1965. This snap was taken of the Rochdale Hornets front-row duo, Peter Birchall and Kevin Ashcroft, before that game looking rather less than impressed at having to represent their country dressed in orange and black!

A new level of international representation was made available to young British players when Under-24 matches were introduced in the mid 'sixties. This came about after a suggestion made by the French Rugby League who were anxious to try out their *"Espoirs"* - a term which translated meant "hopefuls" which, as R.F.L. secretary Bill Fallowfield pointed out in his official programme notes, we in Britain might call promising young players.

Ever the internationalist, Mr. Fallowfield was quick to persuade the Rugby League Council of the benefits of providing such opportunities for our own young players, and so the first Under-24 international took place in April 1965 in Toulouse. Although they won the game 17-9 with a fine performance, all did not run smoothly for the British team as they arrived in France to find their kit had been lost in transit. They had to play the match in a borrowed kit hastily provided by French officials, and it turned out to be the orange and black outfit of the Albi club. British stand-off that day, Phil Kitchin, vividly recalls his teammates being very uncomfortable in the heavy shoulder-padded French jerseys on a very hot day in southern France.

Four Under-24 internationals were played in the 'sixties and always there was confusion over whether the team should be billed as England or Great Britain. The R.F.L. themselves tended towards "England" (as the programme pictured at the top of this page illustrates) yet this was a misnomer as the captain in that very first victory in Toulouse was a Welshman, Mervyn Hicks. And in subsequent years, more Welsh players like Bob Prosser and Clive Sullivan took part, so those who preferred "Great Britain" were actually correct.

The second Under-24 international was played at Oldham under floodlights in October 1966 and, despite this being only a few months after the first game in Toulouse, there were only two survivors in the British side - Les Tonks and Brian Gaines. This clash at the Watersheddings proved to be quite a bloodbath in which referee Eric Lawrinson had his hands full trying to keep control as brawls broke out and fists flew. Great Britain won 12-5, with Roger Millward scoring nine of the points, but all the headlines in the newspapers the following day were about the trouble and some French players' use of the boot.

(Right)
The Batley full-back Stan Gittins dives over for the first try of the night for the Great Britain Under-24s as they walloped France at Castleford in 1969.

(Below)
Keith Davies touches down for one of his hat-trick of tries for the British Under-24s in their 42-2 win over France in 1969. Davies and his fellow Workington Town threequarter, Ian Wright, scored no less than five tries between them as the French boys were left chasing their shadows at Wheldon Road.

In late November 1966, the French "hopefuls" got their only win in what proved to be four attempts in this fixture - a narrow 7-4 scoreline in a match the French used to take the game back to the Basque country by playing it in Bayonne. After a gap of over a year in which the French appeared to lose interest in the fixture, the one they "owed" to the British was staged on a Thursday night at Castleford towards the end of the 1968-69 season, and a brilliant exhibition of attacking play (against a weak and outclassed French side) saw the home team romp to a 42-2 win. Stars of this victory were Stan Gittins, the Batley full-bck, and the Workington Town duo of Keith Davies and Ian Wright in the threequarter line. This Cumbrian duo scored five tries between them, but neither was ever considered for full international honours. The British skills were enjoyed by an audience of several million as the match was televised on the BBC's *"Sportsnight"* programme later the same evening.

Great Britain's Under-24 internationals in the 'sixties

1964-65 season.
Played Saturday, 3rd April 1965 - at Toulouse.
Great Britain beat France 17-9.
G.B. team: Trevor Bedford (Castleford); Rod Tickle (Leigh), Les Thomas (Keighley), Mick Collins (Leigh), Ken Senior (Huddersfield); Phil Kitchin (Whitehaven), Jimmy Boylan (Blackpool); Peter Birchall (Rochdale), Kevin Ashcroft (Rochdale), Les Tonks (Featherstone), Terry Ramshaw (Featherstone), Mervyn Hicks (St.Helens), Doug Laughton (St.Helens). *Substitutes:* Jack Melling (Warrington) and Brian Gaines (Keighley).
Tries: Senior, Boylan, Melling. Goals: Hicks (4).
Referee: Mr. G. Jameau (France).

1965-66 season.
Played Wednesday, 20th October - at Oldham.
Great Britain beat France 12-5.
G.B. team: Colin Tyrer (Leigh); Vaughan Thomas (Featherstone), Terry Major (Hull K.R.), John Maloney (Hull), Bob Wear (Barrow); Roger Millward (Castleford), Bob Prosser (St.Helens); Les Tonks (Featherstone), Kevin Taylor (Oldham), Brian Taylor (Dewsbury), Bill Kirkbride (Workington), Brian Gaines (Keighley), Dave Robinson (Swinton). *Substitutes:* Chris Hesketh (Wigan) and Bob Irving Oldham).
Tries: Wear, Millward. Goals: Millward (3).
Referee: Mr. E. Lawrinson (Warrington).

1966-67 season.
Played Saturday 26th November 1966 - at Bayonne.
France beat Great Britain 7-4.
G.B. team: Colin Tyrer (Leigh); Ian Hare (Widnes), Alan Burwell (Hull K.R.), Jack Gamble (Castleford), Clive Sullivan (Hull); Tommy Warburton (Oldham), Parry Gordon (Warrington); Mick Harrison (Hull), Alan McGlone (Hull), John Stephens (Wigan), Bob Irving (Oldham), Bob Haigh (Wakefield Trinity), Bill Pattinson (Workington). *Substitutes:* Chris Hesketh (Wigan) and Barry Simpson (Swinton).
Goals: Tyrer (2).
Referee: Mr. E. Martung (France).

1968-69 season.
Played Thursday 17th April 1969 - at Castleford.
Great Britain beat France 42-2.
G.B. team: Stan Gittins (Batley); Keith Davies (Workington), Bernard Watson (Leeds), Ian Wright (Workington), Alan Lowndes (Castleford); John Wolford (Bramley), Barry Seabourne (Leeds); Eddie Brown (Rochdale), Mike Stephenson (Dewsbury), Ian Van Bellan (Huddersfield), Mick Redfearn (Castleford), Jimmy Thompson (Featherstone), Kevin O'Loughlin (Wigan). *Substitutes:* Phil Lowe (Hull K.R.) and Vince Farrar (Featherstone).
Tries: Davies (3), Wright (2), Watson, Lowndes, Wolford, O'Loughlin. Goals: Redfearn (4), Wolford (2).
Referee: Mr. W. H. Thompson (Huddersfield).

Great Britain's captains

A total of 14 different captains led Great Britain during the 'Sixties, in the 48 full internationals – both Tests and World Cup matches – they played in the decade.

Eric Ashton dominates this particular honours list, although he played his last international match in 1963. Before that, Ashton had led Great Britain to both the World Cup in 1960 and the Ashes in 1962, and established his place as one of the most decorated British captains in the history of the game. His tally of 13 appearances as Great Britain skipper is more than twice as many as the second on the list, that being the man who replaced him as Test captain in 1963, Tommy Smales.

(Above) Eric Ashton - Great Britain's best

(Above)
Tommy Smales in action in his debut for Great Britain in France in 1962. He first captained his country in the third Test of the 1963 Ashes series, which Britain won in a torrid match with the Aussies at Headingley.

(Below)
Eric Fraser leads Great Britain out to play France at St.Helens in 1961. The Warrington full-back captained his country in three Test matches during the 1960s.

All Great Britain's captains in the 1960s *(with number of games as skipper)*

Eric Ashton   13
Tommy Smales   6
Eric Fraser   3
Alex Murphy   3
Neil Fox 3
Brian Edgar   3
Bill Holliday   3
Bev Risman   3
Jeff Stevenson   2
Derek Turner   2
Harry Poole   2
Alan Hardisty   2
Tommy Bishop   2
Johnny Whiteley   1

(Above) Cumbrian Bill Holliday in action as captain of Great Britain in the 1967 Ashes series versus Australia.

Clubs representation:

Twelve different clubs provided Great Britain captains during the 'Sixties, with Leeds, St.Helens and Wakefield Trinity both having two men lead their country. The British captains and their clubs were: Eric Ashton **(Wigan)**; Tommy Smales **(Huddersfield and Bradford Northern)**; Eric Fraser **(Warrington)**; Alex Murphy **(St.Helens)**; Neil Fox **(Wakefield Trinity)**; Brian Edgar **(Workington Town)**; Bill Holliday **(Hull K.R.)**; Bev Risman **(Leeds)**; Jeff Stevenson **(York)**; Derek Turner **(Wakefield Trinity)**; Harry Poole **(Leeds)**, Alan Hardisty **(Castleford)**, Tommy Bishop **(St.Helens)** and Johnny Whiteley **(Hull)**.

PAPERBACK WRITERS

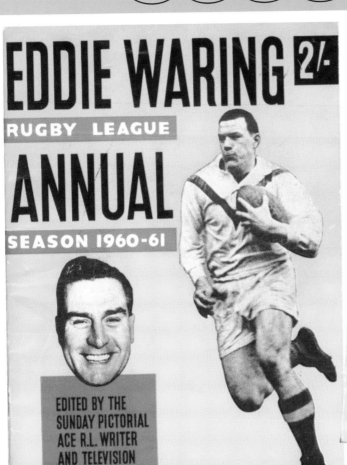

EDDIE WARING 2/-
RUGBY LEAGUE
ANNUAL
SEASON 1960-61

EDITED BY THE
SUNDAY PICTORIAL
ACE R.L. WRITER
AND TELEVISION
COMMENTATOR

FIXTURES * ACTION PICTURES * RECORDS

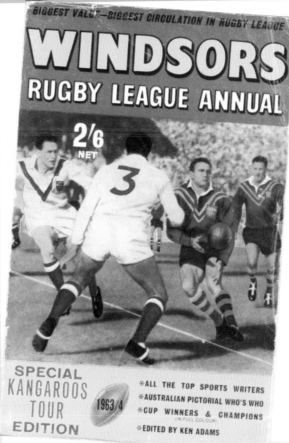

BIGGEST VALUE—BIGGEST CIRCULATION IN RUGBY LEAGUE
WINDSORS
RUGBY LEAGUE ANNUAL
2/6 NET

SPECIAL KANGAROOS TOUR EDITION 1963/4

* ALL THE TOP SPORTS WRITERS
* AUSTRALIAN PICTORIAL WHO'S WHO
* CUP WINNERS & CHAMPIONS (IN FULL COLOUR)
* EDITED BY KEN ADAMS

NEIL FOX

2/6

EDDIE WARING
RUGBY LEAGUE ANNUAL

No. 6   1964-5   2/6

Illustrations of some of Rugby League fans' favourite reading matter in the 1960s, when hardy annuals came in punchy, pocket-sized style, thanks to figureheads like Eddie Waring and Jim Windsor. For the first half of the decade they were rival publications but, by the end of the 'sixties, both had disappeared as the game slipped into its self-induced state of depression. Happily, brochures to celebrate individual player testimonials continued and none better than Neil Fox's.

BEVAN'S CORNER

WILDERSPOOL FAREWELL FOR THE GREATEST TRY-SCORER

(Pictured)
Brian Bevan waves goodbye to the fans at Wilderspool on 23rd April 1962, as the visiting Leigh players congratulate him and join Warringtonians in forming a guard of honour for the game's greatest try-scorer. One young fan with his camera managed to get an exclusive snap of Bevan as he left the field at half-time in a match Warrington went on to win 29-17.

Easter Monday of 1962 was a red-letter day in Rugby League as the game's greatest try-scorer, Brian Bevan, played his last game for Warrington after an incredible career that had spanned 16 seasons in the primrose and blue.

A crowd of 16,478 gathered at Wilderspool on that April day in 1962 to see Bevan's farewell match against Leigh. And they weren't disappointed as the old master scored his 740th and last try for Warrington in typical style with a thrilling dash to the corner flag.

It was the last time Bevan would sit in his famous corner of the Wilderspool dressing room before a competitive match and go through his meticulous pre-game routine which had been his trademark since he joined the Wire way back in 1946. The 'sixties would evolve for Rugby League without the man who had been one of its biggest stars for 16 years, although Bevan did go on to play another season and a half with Blackpool Borough.

(Above) Action at Craven Park in the 1963-64 season as Barrow winger Billy Skeels and hooker Maurice Redhead try to block the path of Whitehaven's Tony Colloby in a north-west "derby." Colloby would, in later years, play for Barrow as well as enjoying a good career with Workington, Salford and Blackpool Borough.

(Above)
Bill Burgess in classic attacking mode versus Hunslet at Craven Park in 1962-63. One of the game's top wingers throughout the 'sixties, Burgess was Barrow's biggest star for most of the decade. Signed from Fylde Rugby Union club for a big fee in 1961, Bill went on to play in 14 Tests for Great Britain (all but one as a Barrow player) and was a member of the 1966 Lions touring team. He also won 11 caps for Lancashire county. Burgess left Barrow when signed by Salford in December 1968 for a £6,000 fee.

Big money Union stars

After being one of the game's top teams in the 1950s, Barrow struggled for much of the early 'sixties. Yet Barrow were happy to spend big money on Rugby Union internationals - first came Engand fly-half Tom Brophy for £6,000 in 1966, and then Barrow paid a massive £14,000 to Welsh wonder-boy Keith Jarrett in September 1969.

(Above) The Barrow team as pictured in the 1967 Challenge Cup Final programme as they went to Wembley. Left to right: *(Back row)*: Maurice Redhead, Ivor Kelland, Brian Backhouse, Mike Watson, Mick Sanderson, Fred Tomlinson, Ray Hopwood, Henry Delooze. *(Front row)*: Bob Wear, Bill Burgess, Tom Brophy, Jim Challinor (captain-coach), Ged Smith, Mike Murray, Harry Hughes. *(Inset)*: Eddie Tees.

(*Above*) **The Batley team in 1961-62 before playing Leigh at Mount Pleasant and wearing a change kit as their visitors also usually wore red and white hoops. Left to right:** (*Standing*): **J.Ireland, P.Fox, C.Sutcliffe, D.Harrison, J.Westbury, A.Dick, N.Field.** (*In front*): **B.Whiteford, M.Shuttleworth, B.Pratt, J.Lawton, R.Astbury and I.Geldard.**

BATLEY FIRST ON TELEVISION

The first match ever to be televised live from Mount Pleasant was on 11th September 1965, when Batley were beaten by Wakefield Trinity 23-7. The game was broadcast by ABC Television and their commentator was Bill Fallowfield, secretary of the Rugby Football League.

Batley favourites in the 'sixties
(*Far left*) Loose-forward Phil Doyle who played for Yorkshire against Cumberland in 1969, becoming Batley's first Yorkshire County man since Norman Field in 1963.
(*Left*) Mighty front-rower Trevor "Tank" Walker who, in 1969-70, set a new record for tries by an open-side prop with 17 touchdowns.

(*Above*)
Norman Field, who became the first post-War Batley player to win a Test cap when he played wing for Great Britain versus Australia at Wembley in 1963. Norman also represented Yorkshire county three times in 1963, including versus the Australians.

Leigh talent boost for the Gallant Youths

Batley produced one of their most successful initiatives of the 'sixties when, after a disappointing start to the 1967-68 season, their scrum-half Terry Gorman identified several amateur players in his home town of Leigh whom he believed would help strengthen the "Gallant Youths" side if given the opportunity. Terry was an experienced footballer who had played previously for both Huddersfield and Wakefield, and he proved to be a good judge of talent.

Of the half a dozen or so he recommended, the first to sign was a young full-back from Tyldesley Rugby Union club called Stan Gittins. Following trials under the name of "Jones" he signed for Batley and became the youngest player to make his first team debut for the club when he appeared against Wigan at Central Park on 9th October 1967 just after his 17th birthday. Stan Gittins quickly became a big favourite at Mount Pleasant and went on to win Great Britain Under-24 honours.

Two more backs followed Gittins to Batley, John Morris and John Cooke, plus a forward colleague of Cooke's at Leigh Miners Welfare, Tommy Martyn.

Terry Gorman certainly did Batley a good turn with these players, and helped launched the professional career of Tommy Martyn who went on to be a full Great Britain international.

BLACKPOOL B.

(Above) The Blackpool team for the 1966 Lancashire Cup semi-final versus Oldham. Left to right: *(Standing):* Bob Rippon (kitman), Jim Belshaw, Roger Dufty, Albert Seddon, Alan Whitworth, Mick Ducie, Brian Winstanley, John Farrell, Frank Sullivan. *(In front):* Brian Olsen, Brian Holmes, Martin Dickens (captain), Johnny Fairhurst, Norman Ince, Tex McCarrick and Jimmy Gee.

(Above) Blackpool Borough always provided a haven for many players from Wigan, among them several top former internationals. This picture shows David Bolton leading out the Borough, followed by Ray Ashby, as Blackpool played a re-arranged match versus Leigh actually at Central Park, under floodlights in January 1969.

Boro' the pioneers

Blackpool Borough were the pioneers of Rugby League in the 'sixties as they built their own brand new town centre stadium, Borough Park. It opened at the start of the 1963-64 season.

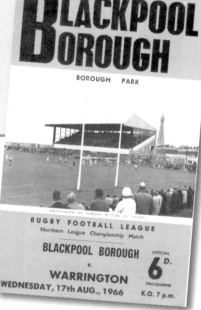

(Left) There's no doubt that Tommy Bishop was the best player to be produced by Blackpool Borough. They signed him from junior rugby in St.Helens and saw him develop into one of the world's top scrum-halves. This picture is from 1961 and shows Tommy trying to evade the determined Rochdale Hornets loose-forward Jim Parr.

BRADFORD N.

(Above) Bradford Northern scrum-half Tommy Smales and loose-forward Johnny Rae practice their scrum-base move in daylight training at Odsal before the 1965 Yorkshire Cup Final.

Northern's revival

It remains one of the pivotal stories of Rugby League in the 'Sixties, the way Bradford Northern dropped out of the game in 1963-64 season, unable to carry on after gates had slipped to as low as 300 in the vast Odsal bowl. But their revival, led by Joe Phillips and Trevor Foster, saw Northern become one of the best supported clubs in the game in the second half of the 'sixties. A crowd of 13,542 attended their first 'reborn' fixture in August 1964 (v. Hull K.R.)

(Above) Dave Stockwell in possession for Bradford as they played Featherstone at Odsal in 1967. Bak Diabira is the man in support - both Stockwell and Diabira were great crowd favourites at the heart of Northern's team.
(Left) Another victory in the Headingley Sevens as Alan Rhodes receives the Wills Trophy in 1966 from Mrs. Gordon Thomas

(Pictured) The reformed Bradford Northern wasted no time in getting their first trophy in the Odsal cabinet, winning the inagural Sevens tournament at Headingley in early August 1964. Their team was: *(Left to right):* Derek Carr, Brian Lord, Idwal Fisher, Keith Williams (captain), Johnny Rae, Ian Brooke, Mike Brown and Brian Todd.

BRAMLEY

(Above) Bramley winger Heap is tackled by Greatorex of Featherstone Rovers at the Barley Mow as the two Yorkshire rivals met in September 1964.

FIRST MEDALS FOR BRAMLEY

*Bramley got the first medals in their history in 1962, thanks to celebrity supporter Jim Windsor who had the gold medals specially struck to mark their achievement of attaining First Division status.

(Above)
Bramley forward Jubb on the charge against Blackpool Borough at the Barley Mow in April 1964. The Blackpool defender is Berry.

A NEW HOME

*Bramley, nicknamed "The Villagers" moved sideways from the Barley Mow to a brand new ground in 1966. The new grandstand at McLaren Field cost £35,000.

From the scrapbook: The Bramley team pictured in 1962. Left to right: (Standing): Tommy Parker, Norman Bastian, Alan Jubb, Terry Robbins, David Horn, Brian Larkin, Terry Hollindrake. (In front): Alf Barron, Denis Morgan, Brian Wrigglesworth, John Wolford, Jack Rogers and Stan Smith.

Bramley got a new look to go with their move to a new ground and in 1967 the former Wakefield Trinity scrum-half Keith Holliday (above) was their player-coach as they took on Leeds at McLaren Field. Leeds forward Albert Eyre watches closely.

CASTLEFORD

Castleford Rugby League Football Club
LIMITED

CASTLEFORD v YORK
Monday, 11th October, 1965   Kick-off 7.30 p.m.

Official Programme - Sixpence

Three of the major figures in Castleford's success of the late 'sixties. *(Left to right):* Dennis Hartley, Alan Hardisty (both pictured in the 1969 Wembley win over Salford) and Malcolm Reilly (pictured trying to evade Wakefield scrum-half Joe Bonnar in the 1969 Cup semi-final at Headingley.)

(Above) The Castleford team in the spring of 1964, just as the "Classy Cas" momentum was beginning to roll and they were to become one of the most fashionable sides of the 'sixties. Left to right: *(Standing):* Doug Walton, John Clark, Jack Hirst, Andrew Johnson, Geoff Ward, John Sheridan, Frank Smith. *(In front):* Johnny Ward, Derek Edwards, Alan Hardisty (captain), Roy Bell, Keith Howe and Ken Foulkes. *(Missing: Keith Hepworth).*

DEWSBURY

(Left)
The Dewsbury team in 1967 as they headed for their second Challenge Cup semi-final in successive years. Left to right: *(Back row)*: **Brian Taylor, Colin Cook, Geoff Tolson, Jim Naylor, Trevor Lowe, David Blakeley.** *(Middle row)*: **Willie Walker, Brian Firth, Alvin Newall (captain), Garth Budge, Geoff Marsh.** *(In front)*: **Trevor Ward, Alan Edwards, Peter Coates and Roy Firth.**

Crown Flatt cup magic

The magic of the Cup had Dewsbury under its spell in both 1966 and '67 as the boys from Crown Flatt went achingly close to a Wembley Final. Two consecutive semi-finals saw Dewsbury lose, first to St.Helens 12-5, and the following year to Barrow 14-9. The appeal of the Cup was shown when a crowd of 13,527 packed Crown Flatt for the 1967 tie versus Salford *(see picture, below.)*

THE RUGBY FOOTBALL LEAGUE
Challenge Cup Semi-Final
DEWSBURY v ST. HELENS
SATURDAY
16th APRIL
1966
AT
STATION ROAD
SWINTON
Kick-off 2.30 p.m.
OFFICIAL SOUVENIR PROGRAMME - 1/-

(Above) **Dewsbury's Colin Cook on the attack in the 1967 cup tie with Salford.**

(Above)
Dewsbury winger Geoff Marsh shows his paces against Bradford Northern at Odsal, as Aussie Lionel Williamson and Welsh full-back Terry Price do their best to keep up. Marsh played in both the 1966 and '67 Cup semi-finals.

(Above) The Dons team which beat Halifax in front of 2,300 people at Tatters Field in April 1962. Left to right: (Standing): Alan Hepworth, Bernard Asquith, Malcolm Kirk, Keith Davies, George Goodyear, Frank Bowers. (In front): Brian Saville, Eric Lockwood, Derek Woodfield, Kevin Doyle (captain), Ted Heath, Peter Goodchild and Brian Tasker.

(Pictured, right: "The Dons of Tatters Field" was published in 1962 to celebrate the completion of Doncaster's first ten seasons in the League. (Far right, above): Peter Goodchild, Doncaster's Yorkshire county winger, tackled by Berwyn Jones of Wakefield. (Far right, below): Brian Saville signs for the Dons from Hull in 1962, watched by Chairman Len Tattersfield and director Dennis Speakman.

(Left)
The Dons in 1962 getting a pre-match pep talk from their coach Bryn Goldswain. The Welshman , who hailed from Swansea, proved to be the Doncaster club's longest serving coach in the 'sixties, being at the helm for four seasons from 1960 to 1964. Among the players listening closely to Bryn's words are: Alan Hepworth, Peter Goodchild, Brian Saville and Kevin Doyle.

(Right)
Malcolm Dixon leads the Rovers down the Wembley steps with the Challenge Cup in 1967, followed by Lance Todd Trophy winner Carl Dooler.
(Below)
Rovers coach Laurie Gant is held shoulder high by his players with the Cup at Wembley in 1967.

Aussies beaten
One of many great days for the Rovers of Featherstone in the 'sixties came when they beat the 1963 Australian tourists 23-17. A Wednesday afternoon crowd of 7,850 were there to see Rovers repeat their 1959 success over the Aussies.

Gary Cooper on the attack as Rovers beat the Kangaroos in 1963.

(Left) The Rovers team which played Wakefield on 20th January 1962, before a record crowd for a League match at Post Office Road of 14,990. Left to right:
(Standing): Gary Waterworth, Colin Clift, Cliff Lambert, Terry Clawson, Don Fox, Gary Jordan, Len Hammill.
(In front): Willis Fawley, Joe Mullaney, Ken Greatorex, Norman Hockley, Jack Fennell, Jim Hunt.

(Above) One of Johnny Freeman's 290 tries for Halifax. Always a big favourite of the Thrum Hall crowd, Johnny was a link between the great team of the 1950s and the success that followed in the 'sixties leading up to the Championship in 1965 - he retired in 1967.

(Below) Ronnie James in action in the 1965 Championship Final. The Welsh full-back from Maesteg made his Halifax debut in 1961 and went on to kick 1,028 goals for the club in his 10-year career.

Thrum Hall

Under lights

(Above) A floodlit night at Thrum Hall in October 1968 as Halifax forward Jack Scroby tries to power his way past Leeds centre Syd Hynes.

(Above) The image forever etched into the history of the Halifax club from the 1960s, as their captain John Burnett - a local lad from Pellon - proudly lifts the Rugby League Championship trophy in 1965. Halifax had just beaten St.Helens 15-7 in the Final at Swinton's Station Road and *(below)* the whole team join Burnett in the celebration. It was Halifax's first Championship title since 1907.

(Above) Peter Ramsden flings out a pass in Fartown's victory over Wakefield in the 1962 Championship Final at Odsal Stadium. Huddersfield won 14-5 to take the title, and (above, right) skipper Tommy Smales holds the famous old trophy aloft.

Fartown's Scots & Sevens

No club in Rugby League had a stronger link with the Scottish borders, and the list of Scots to don the claret and gold colours was long and distinguished - none better, of course, than Great Britain's inaugral World Cup leader Dave Valentine. Another, Alex Fiddes, was a major influence in introducing Sevens to Rugby League and (right) "From the scrapbook" we see Rob Valentine chaired by Don Close after Huddersfield's triumph in the 1967 Leeds Sevens at Headingley.

HUDDERSFIELD
Cricket and Athletic Club

— OFFICIAL —
Nº 7565   Football Programme

Huddersfield v. Widnes
Saturday, November 3rd, 1962

(Above)
Huddersfield's fine tradition of producing good R.L. literature was maintained during the 'sixties.

(Above) Huddersfield in 1961-62, reached both the Challenge Cup and Championship Finals in a year to remember for Fartown. Left to right: (Standing): Eddie Strong, Don Close, Aiden Breen, Mike Wicks, Brian Rowe, Mick Clark, Ken Bowman, Ken Noble, Ted Slevin. (Seated): Ray Haywood, Leo Booth, Frank Dyson, Gwyn Davies, Tommy Smales (captain), Peter Ramsden, Harry Deighton and Geoff Stocks.

(Left)
Arthur Keegan and coach Johnny Whiteley compare notes before a training session.
(Below)
Hull F.C. entertained New Zealand at the Boulevard in 1965 - the Kiwis won 11-8.

NEW ZEALAND TOUR 1965
BOULEVARD GROUND, HULL
SATURDAY, 9th OCTOBER

HULL

VERSUS

NEW ZEALAND

Nº 4755   OFFICIAL SOUVENIR PROGRAMME   6d.

(Above)
Clive Sullivan, who went on to captain Great Britain, on the attack for Hull versus Hunslet, with Terry Hollindrake close by.

(Above) After all their success in the 1950s, Hull F.C. found the early years of the 'sixties much more difficult. This early 1960s team features, on the back row: Jim Drake, Cyril Sykes, Bill Drake, Terry Hollindrake, Peter Bateson, David Doyle-Davidson and Keith Barnwell. Among the players on the front row alongside captain Mick Scott are scrum-half Tommy Finn and stand-off George Matthews, recruited from the Barrow area.

HULL K.R.

(Right) All aboard the *"Cornish Express."* Graham Paul, Hull Kingston Rovers' flying winger from Penzance, on the attack for the Robins in 1963 against Wigan at Central Park.

(Above) Phil Lowe became a powerful presence in the Robins second-row in the late 'sixties whilst still a teenager. *(Right)* Hull K.R. in change kit at Craven Park in the 1962-63 season. Left to right: *(Standing):* Robin Coverdale, John Taylor, Brian Tyson, Mike Blackmore, Bob Harris, Les Chamberlain, Terry Major, Jim Drake. *(In front):* Brian Hatch, Peter Flanagan, Cyril Kellett, Graham Paul and David Elliott.

(Above) The Robins in April, 1967, captained by mighty Frank Foster and established as a real force in the game. Left to right: *(Standing):* Brian Tyson, John Moore, Eric Palmer, Frank Fox, Bill Holliday, Mike Blackmore, Terry Major, Cyril Kellett. *(Seated):* Arthur Bunting, Chris Young, David Elliott, Frank Foster, Roger Millward, Alan Burwell and Peter Flanagan. Rovers had won the Yorkshire Cup earlier in the 1966-67 season.

(Above) The Hunslet team pictured at Parkside in the 1964-65 season. Left to right: *(Standing):* Geoff Gunney, Cliff Taylor, Billy Baldwinson, Fred Ward (captain-coach), Dennis Hartley, John Griffiths, Bernard Prior. *(In front):* Brian Gabbitas, Alan Preece, Geoff Shelton, Alan Marchant, Barry Lee, Billy Langton. *(Insets)* Bill Ramsey and Ken Eyre.

(Right)
Hunslet boys at Wembley in the epic Cup Final with Wigan in 1965. In the picture are: Alan Marchant, Bill Ramsey, Dennis Hartley, Barry Lee, Ken Eyre, Geoff Gunney and skipper Fred Ward. The sole Wiganer is blindside prop Brian McTigue.

(Above) **International forward Geoff Gunney in possession for Hunslet in the 1965 Cup sem-final win over Wakefield Trinity. Geoff was synonymous with the Hunslet club throughout the 'sixties, as was their programme *"The Parksider."***

Hunslet's G.B. Test stars

Hunslet was famed as a great breeding ground of talented Rugby League players and the successes of the Parkside club were always built on local lads. Some progressed even further, and in the 'sixties, as well as the well known figure of Geoff Gunney, other Hunslet boys Geoff Shelton (centre) and Bill Ramsey (second-row) became Great Britain internationals. Both toured with the 1966 Lions team after playing at Wembley for Hunslet in the 1965 Cup Final.

Geoff Shelton playing for Hunslet vesus Hull at Parkside.

(Above)
John Smallwood, the chairman and major power broker of the Keighley club in the 'sixties. He was appointed the Rugby League Council chairman for the 1967-68 season and was manager of the Great Britain team at the 1968 World Cup.

(Above) The Keighley team at Whitehaven early in the 1967-68 season, captained by ex-Wakefield Trinity full-back Don Metcalfe, and including Lawkholme Lane favourites like Dave Worthy, Bill Aspinall, Terry O'Brien and Eric Palmer.

Geoff the 1966 Lion

Prop Geoff Crewdson became the first Lions tourist from Keighley in 1966. *(Above)* Geoff is congratulated on his selection by club chairman, Mr. Norman Mitchell and his team-mates - this was before playing Bramley in March '66.

(Above)
On a misty day at Lawkholme Lane in the 1962-63 season, Bryan Todd dives over to score against promotion rivals Hunslet (no video replays in those days!) The Keighley team pictured *(right)* went on to win promotion in that season, finishing as runners-up to Hunslet.

(Above) Keighley in 1962-63. Left to right: *(Standing):* Jack Taylor (physio.), Billy Watson (kitman), Harry Plunkett, Albert Eyre, Barry Anderson, Vince Jackson, Geoff Crewdson, Kenny Pye, Frank Haigh, Gordon Brown (coach). *(In front):* Alfie Barron, Bryan Todd, Roy Bleasby, Garfield Owen (captain), Barry Jackson and Roy Sabine.

(Left) **The Loiners who won the Championship in 1960-61. Left to right:** (Standing): **Ken Thornett, Don Robinson, Lewis Jones (captain), Dennis Goodwin, Jack Fairbank, Brian Shaw, Robbins.** (In front): **Barry Simms, Wilf Rosenberg, Derek Hallas, Colin Evans, Delmas Hodgkinson and Fred Pickup.**

(Right) A touch of silverware for Leeds Football Chairman Jack Myerscough to celebrate at the end of 1966-67 season, as club captain Harry Poole and centre Dick Gemmell hold aloft the League Leaders trophy and the Yorkshire League cup, after being presented by Mr. Jack Harding, the RFL Chairman.

Loiners fans celebration

Throughout the 'sixties the Leeds Supporters' Club annual handbook *"The Headingley Leeder"* was a popular feature for all fans of the Loiners. Their Supporters' Club, founded in 1948, did much sterling work for the game, led by such enthusiastic long serving officials as Joe Wager and Harry Falkingham. And those Leeds fans had much to enjoy in their 1969 handbook as they celebrated

Leeds' second Championship winning season under Joe Warham as coach. Captained by Barry Seabourne they had also won the Yorkshire Cup in '68.

(Above) Eddie Ratcliffe was a loyal servant to Leeds throughout the 'sixties, who bided his time in the "A" team for long periods but never let the Loiners down.

(Left)
A Rugby League legend arrived as the new coach at Leigh in 1961-2 in the shape of Alan Prescott, the ex-Great Britain captain and hero of the 1958 Ashes win. Here, Prescott is welcomed to Hilton Park by, among others, Leigh players Stan Owen, Walmsley, Bill Robinson, Danny Harris, Humble and Bev Risman.

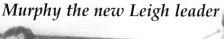

Murphy the new Leigh leader

Alex in an early game for Leigh at Hilton Park versus Widnes.

From the scrapbook ... The Leigh team on 4th February 1967. Left to right: (Standing): Rod Tickle, Colin Tyrer, Tony Davies, John McVay, Mick Murphy, Bob Welding, Derek Higgs. (In front): Joe Walsh, Mick Collins, Wilf Briggs, Gordon Lewis, Charlie Winslade and Tommy Grainey.

Leigh the big spenders

Leigh were never afraid to "flash the cash" in the 1960s in their search for stars, just as they had done in the previous decade. They got their fingers burnt with four South Africans in 1960-61, none of whom made it, and then paid a record £6,000 fee to international Rugby Union fly-half Bev Risman to turn professional.

(Left) Three international prop-forwards in action at Hilton Park as Leigh played Workington in 1962, but only one was a native Leyther - Town's Norman Herbert. The Leigh man in possession is Bill Robinson (a Wiganer) watched closely by big Stan Owen (a Welshman.)

LIVERPOOL CITY

(*Above*) Liverpool City director Dr. Harry Roebuck, who became Chairman of the Rugby League Council for the 1963-64 season.

From the scrapbook ... Liverpool City winger Eddie McDonnell on the attack versus Huddersfield at Fartown in the 1965-66 season. Backing up is City scrum-half Jeff Heaton.

(*Above*) Wilf Hunt, one of the great figures in the history of Liverpool City. He gave eleven years' service to City, playing up to 1966, during which he set new career records for the club of 304 goals and 731 points.

(*Right*) Liverpool City in the early 'sixties, captained by full-back Ray Ashby, who went on to be City's only full Great Britain Test cap when he played versus France in 1964.

Huyton - a new name in the game

The only new name to appear among the list of Northern Rugby League member clubs during the 'sixties was Huyton. They took over the mantle from Liverpool City as the game's professional club in Merseyside in 1968-69, but it wasn't until the start of the following season - in August 1969 - that their brand new ground at Alt Park was ready for action.

The green and white colours of the much liked old Liverpool City club were replaced by the amber, red and black of Huyton, as the new boys officially opened Alt Park with a match against Salford, then the emerging glamour team of the league (*see the programme for that match, illustrated right.*) The President of the Rugby League, and also Patron of Huyton R.L.F.C., Lord Derby, did the honours. In that programme, the club chairman Bill Whittaker wrote: "*Our ups and downs through the years have been many, but we have learned that the spirit of sport is unquenchable ... our spirit and pride today as we see the wonderful hand-gained facilities spreading over Alt Park is unbounding. We believe there is a future for Rugby League here in Huyton and district ... and all the people here today can see for themselves.*"

HUYTON R.L.F.C.
ALT PARK
HUYTON

HUYTON
v
SALFORD

SUNDAY AUGUST 10th 1969
at ALT PARK HUYTON
Kick-off 3·00 p.m.
ADMISSION BY PROGRAMME ONLY 5/-

MISS ANNABEL
HIGH CLASS FLORIST   FLOWER ARRANGEMENTS BY EXPERTS
5 SHERBOURNE SQUARE, HUYTON TOWN CENTRE. Phone 061 489 8676

(Right) One of the most bizarre signings of the 'sixties by Oldham was that of the international shot-put champion Arthur Rowe in 1962. He didn't hang around very long and in his "A" team debut, coach Frank Dyson had to point the way for him.

Bob Irving - an Oldham hero

For much of 1960s Oldham struggled to match their illustrious achievements of the 'fifties. Yet, they had one remarkable player who was a Great Britain international whilst still a teenager and who was consistently one of the most respected forwards in the game. Bob Irving was only 16-years-old when he was recruited by Oldham from the St.Joesph's amateur club in Huddersfield in January 1965. Within a few weeks he made his first team debut, and rapidly found himself capped for both Great Britain Under-24s and Yorkshire county. At the age of 18, Bob made his Test debut in the 1967 Ashes series against Australia and went on to be a member of the victorious 1970 Lions touring team. A true Oldham hero he played a total of 296 games for the Roughyeds in his eight years at the Watersheddings.

(Above) An 11,338 crowd saw Oldham lose 12-4 to the 1963 Kangaroo tourists - and both Trevor Simms and Johnny Noon had their hands full trying to stop the Aussie winger Ken Irvine.

(Above) The Oldham team line up at the end of the 1963-64 season with Second Division championship trophy - there was to be no promotion for them, however, as the two divisional system had already been scrapped. The other trophy is the pre-season Law Cup. The players are, left to right: (Standing): Harry Major, Vince Nestor, Johnny Noon, Ken "Tug" Wislon, Charlie Bott, Trevor Simms, Stuart Whitehead, Dave Parker, Geoff Robinson. (Seated): Peter Smethurst, Geoff Sims, Frank Dyson (captain-coach), John Donovan, Mike Elliott and Brian Lord.

ROCHDALE H.

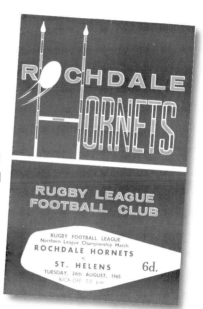

Johnny Noon, as featured in this programme *(right)* from August 1965. He was in his second year as Hornets coach.

(Above) **Rochdale hooker Kevin Ashcroft gets to grips with Keighley's Bill Aspinall at the Athletic Grounds.**

(Left)
The Hornets team in 1965-66, the season they reached the Lancashire Cup Final. Left to right:
(Standing): **Mike Hope, Jack Gregory, Tony Pratt, Stan Owen, Ken Parr, Apisia Toga, Kevin Ashcroft.** *(Seated):* **Peter Birchall, Joe Chamberlain, Syd Miller, Johnny Noon (captain-coach), John Fishwick and Graham Starkey.**

Rochdale Hornets and the colourful Fijian adventure

One of Rugby League's most unlikely adventures in the 1960s was the signing of several Fijian Rugby Union players by Rochdale Hornets. First came two of the greatest stars in Fijian rugby history, Joe Levula and Orisi Dawai, and they were followed by giant forwards Laitia Ravouvou and Voate Drui. Later came the very talented Apisia Toga. Numerous other Fijians followed, both to Hornets and other clubs, but the Lancashire cotton town of Rochdale will always be best associated with the Fijians. They brought a new excitement to the game in some of its more difficult times the 'sixties, and certainly at Rochdale the Fijians were really taken to the hearts of the local fans. Names like Joe Levula and Toga have never been forgotten.

(Above) **Joe Levula of Rochdale**

SALFORD

(Right)
A Salford line-up from 1966, just before the revolution inspired by Chairman Brian Snape began to take shape.
Left to right: *(Standing):* Les Bettinson, Alan Dorning, Terry Ogden, Mick Henighan, Jeff Smart , Mick Clarke, Terry Wilson. *(In front):* Paul Murphy, Joe Southward, Arthur Hughes, John Sims, Trevor Rabbit and Mark Taylor.

Salford's 'sixties spending spree

Three who served the Red Devils well in the 1960s - Les Bettinson, Jackie Brennan and Peter Smethurst.

(Above) **Colin Dixon of Salford grabbed by Alan Hardisty of Castleford in the 1969 Cup Final at Wembley.**

Salford were revolutionised in the second half of the 'sixties thanks to the enterprise and ambition of their Chairman Brian Snape. With the arrival of floodlit rugby at the Willows in 1966, followed by the new Variety Centre, Salford became the most fashionable of Rugby League clubs. And on the field the "Red Devils" spending spree brought a host of new players to Salford - between 1966 and the end of 1968, around £70,000 had been paid out and among the new recruits were: Charlie Bott, Chris Hesketh, Alan McInnes, Ken Halliwell, Mike Kelly, Jim Mills, Malcolm Price, Peter Smethurst, Arthur Hughes, Mike Coulman, David Watkins, Bill Burgess and Colin Dixon.

OFFICIAL PROGRAMME
SALFORD FOOTBALL CLUB
6ᴰ

(Left)
This was the programme Salford fans would enjoy at the Willows in the 1965-66 season.

ST.HELENS

(*Above*) Alex Murphy practices feeding the scrum during floodlit training at Knowsley Road with his front-row forwards: John Warlow, Bob Dagnall and John Tembey.

Voll's farewell

The great South African Tom Van Vollenhoven picked up his last major trophy when he captained Saints to the Lancashire Cup in 1967. He retired at the end of the '67-68 season. With him are Kel Coslett and Eric Chisnall.

(*Above*)
Dick Huddart about to use his famous hand-off for Saints against Swinton at Station Road in 1963.

(*Below*)
The Lions were on the receiving end again as Peter Harvey touches down for a St.Helens try

(*Left*)
The Saints in 1961. Left to right: (*Standing*): Dick Huddart, Cliff Watson, Tom Van Vollenhoven, Abe Terry, Bob Dagnall, Don Vines. (*Seated*): John Donovan, Frank Barrow, Mick Sullivan, Vince Karalius (captain), Alex Murphy, Wilf Smith, Brian McGinn. (*Missing:* Ken Large and Austin Rhodes.)

The Swinton team in 1965 - just a year after the second of their successive Championship triumphs, but already with several new young faces in their ranks as the Lions again saw their Wembley dream dashed, this time by Wigan in the Cup semi-final. This team is, left to right: *(Standing):* Barry Simpson, Ken Halliwell, Dave Robinson, Harold Bate, Graham Rees, Derek Clarke. *(Seated):* Albert Cartwright, Frank Eckersley, Bob Fleet, Ken Gowers (captain), Alan Buckley, Billy 'Daz' Davies and John Stopford.

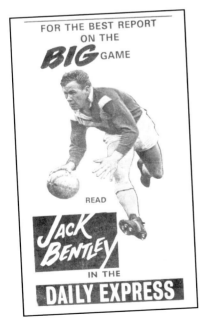

((*Above*) Swinton's George Parkinson featured in this 1965 'Daily Express' advert.

(*Above*) John Speed, the aptly named winger who starred in Swinton's Championship winning teams of 1963 and '64 as part of the famous three-quarter line: Speed, Fleet, Buckley and Stopford.

Bob's bonus as Swinton won Lancashire Cup

Swinton finally got their hands on the Lancashire Cup in 1969 after four lost finals earlier in the decade - and there was a little bonus for their captain, Bob Fleet *(pictured with the trophy.)* At half-time in the 1969 Final against Leigh, when the scores were level, opposing skipper Alex Murphy bet Bob a fiver that his Leigh team would win the cup. The Lions went on to win 11-2 to take the Lancashire Cup back to Station Road. True to his word, Alex did pay up, so the Swinton captain went home with £45, whilst his team-mates had to settle for the £40 winning money.

WAKEFIELD TRINITY

(Left) Wakefield Trinity line up before playing Hunslet at Parkside, in 1964.
Left to right: *Standing):* Geoff Oakes, Jack Wilkinson, Bob Haigh, John Bell, David Sampson, Keith Holliday, Gerry Round. *(In front):* Gert Coetzer, Don Vines, Derek Turner (captain), Ian Brooke, Ken Hirst and Colin Greenwood.

(Above) Trinity at Wembley in 1962 - Jack Wilkinson and Neil Fox bring down a Huddersfield opponent.

(Above) Newspaper caricatures of Wakefield Trinity players Don Fox, David Jeanes, Ken Batty and Gert Coetzer as they headed to both the Championship and Challenge Cup Finals in consecutive weeks in 1968.

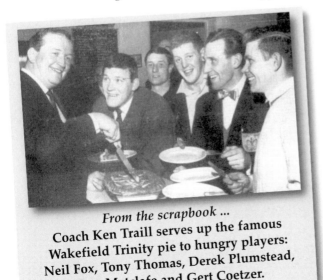

From the scrapbook ...
Coach Ken Traill serves up the famous Wakefield Trinity pie to hungry players: Neil Fox, Tony Thomas, Derek Plumstead, Don Metclafe and Gert Coetzer.

(Left) John Etty with the Challenge Cup in 1960. Part of that fine Trinity three-quarter line with Fred Smith, Neil Fox and Alan Skene as they romped to Wembley glory, Etty had been a bargain £500 buy from Oldham but proved to be a great asset to Wakefield.

(*Above*) - Willie Aspinall flies high to score a try versus Wakefield Trinity in 1966, the year in which he went on tour to Australia with the Lions.

Warrington hosted the opening fixture for both Kangaroo tours of the 'sixties. In 1963, a crowd of over 20,000 were at Wilderspool to see the Australians win 28-20. The picture (*above*) shows Wire Charlie Winslade in a wrestle for the ball with Aussie forwards Ian Walsh and Noel Kelly involved

(*Above*)
Brian Glover and Bobby Greenhough in action for the Wire in the 1961-62 season. Glover gave fine service throughout the decade at Wilderspool.

(*Above*) The Warrington team in 1963. Left to right: (*Standing*): Laurie Gilfedder, Bill Payne, Brian Glover, Eric Fraser, Clarke, Henry Delooze, Brian Catterall, Charlie Winslade. (*In front*): Bobby Greenhough, Alistair Brindle, Keith Holden, Jim Challinor (captain), Joe Pickavance.

WHITEHAVEN

(Above) Bill Holliday leading Whitehaven to victory over Wigan in the 1964-65 season - soon after Holliday was signed by Hull K.R. in a deal which rescued Whitehaven financially. The other 'Haven forwards in the picture are Les Moore and Jim Wilson (ex-Barrow).

Top of the League

For clubs like Whitehaven, who didn't win major honours, moments of glory were few and far between in the 'sixties. A record crowd in 1960 and a win over the Kiwis in 1965 were savoured; but best of all was seeing 'Haven stand on the very top of the Rugby League for a couple of weeks in 1969 - a famous win over Warrington confirming that position and Whitehaven's joy.

(Above) **Whitehaven's Jim Powe and Tom Gainford chase down Warrington in 1969.**

(Above)
Alex Cassie dives over to score for Whitehaven in the 1968-69 season. A Scotsman, Cassie was signed from Melrose in 1962 and gave over a decade's excellent service to 'Haven, playing 288 first team games.

(Left)
The Whitehaven team in the latter part of the 1961-62 season, before playing Halifax at Thrum Hall. Left to right: (Standing): Tex Bailiffe, Bill Holliday, Jim Neale, Jim Lynch, Jim Hewitson, Les Moore, Colin Byrne. (In front): Harry Hughes, Brian Shillinglaw, Phil Kitchin, George Baker, Louis Shepherd and Joe Mossop.

(Left)
Widnes, the Challenge Cup winners in 1964. Left to right:
(Standing): Edgar Bate, Jim Measures, Frank Collier, Wally Hurstfield, Arthur Hughes, Bob Randall, Johnny Gaydon.
(Seated): George Kemel, Bob Chisnall, Alan Briers, Vince Karalius (captain), Frank Myler, Bill Thompson, Ged Lowe.
(In front): Ray Owen and Ged Smith.

Chemics Cup marathon

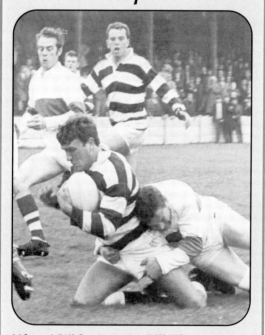

(Above) **Widnes centre Bill Thompson tackled against Liverpool City in a real Merseyside derby.**

When Widnes beat Liverpool City 16-6 at Naughton Park in the second round of the Challenge Cup in 1964, it was the only round they were able to successfully negotiate without a replay on their way to ultimate success at Wembley. The Chemics played a total of nine games to get to Wembley, including five replays.

Frank Myler ranks as one of the greatest rugby players ever to be produced by Widnes, his home town club. Frank was a World Cup winner in 1960 and twice a Lions tourist. The picture *(right)* shows Myler on the run for Widnes in the 1962 Western Championship Final versus Workington as Town centre John O'Neill covers across.

(Above) **Following a pass from Jim Measures, Frank Collier bounds over for a try versus Hull K.R. at Wembley in 1964 which helped him with the Lance Todd Trophy.**

(Left)
The Wigan team which played Salford on 11th April 1966. Left to right: (Standing): David Stephens, Tom Woosey, Brian McTigue, Geoff Lyon, Harry Major, Colin Clarke, Tony Stephens, Laurie Gilfedder. (Seated): Kevin O'Loughlin, Bill Francis, Trevor Lake, Eric Ashton (captain), Frankie Parr, Ray Ashby and Chris Hesketh.

(Left) A try for Billy Boston at Central Park versus Leeds. Billy played his last game for Wigan in April 1968 - before heading briefly for Blackpool Borough.

(Left)
Pictured here as a 19-year-old, hooker Colin Clarke went on to play 15 seasons for Wigan.

(Above) Monty meets Mac.
Chief guest at Wembley in 1963, Lord Montgomery, meets the Wigan team, who were wearing their nifty Litesome tracksuits. "Monty" is introduced to Brian McTigue by skipper Eric Ashton, as Frank Collier looks on with a smile. Local Wigan lad McTigue was one of the best ever ball-handling forwards.

Wigan enjoy Wembley victory in 1965

After two unsuccessful visits to Wembley in 1961 and 1963 (in which they lost to St.Helens and Wakefield respectively) Wigan finally got their name on the Challenge Cup again in the 'sixties after beating Hunslet in the 1965 thriller. (Above) The Wigan players enjoy their lap of honour at Wembley with half-backs Cliff Hill and Frankie Parr carrying the trophy, followed by: Trevor Lake, Roy Evans, Ray Ashby, Laurie Gilfedder, Danny Gardiner and Keith Holden.

WORKINGTON T.

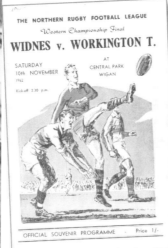

(Above) Harry Archer, master baker who cooked up a great half-back partnership with Sol Roper - plus the programme from the 1962 Western Championship Final against Widnes when Town got their silverware.

Town's sevens title

(Above) John "Sol" Roper dives over for a try for Workington Town in a West Cumbrian derby in the early 'sixties with Whitehaven's Dave Hazeldon in close pursuit. "Sol" had captained Workington at Wembley in 1958 and was a key part of their successes in the 1960s, for several years rated one of the best un-capped scrum-halves in the game. In 1967 Roper was allowed to leave Workington and join Whitehaven where he eventually became player-coach. He returned to Derwent Park to play in Cumberland's famous win over Australia in 1967.

(Above) Workington forwards Malcolm Moss and "Spanky" McFarlane lift the National Sevens trophy in February 1969, won in a snowstorm at Swinton and broadcast live on BBC television.

(Right)
Workington Town in 1962. Left to right: *(Back row)*: Billy Ivison (coach), Danny Gardiner, Bill Martin, Matt McLeod, Malcolm Moss, Tom McNally, John O'Neill, official. *(Middle row)*: John Short (physio.), Japie Ferreira, Harry Archer, Brian Edgar (captain), Sol Roper, Piet Pretorius, John Wilson (skipman). *(In front)*: Benny Eve and Syd Lowden.

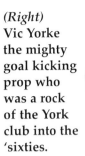

From the scrapbook ... the York team in 1963-64.
Left to right: (Standing): V.Yorke, G.Smith, G.Steel,
D.Lamming, W.Hargreaves, C.Evans, J.Elmer, A.Firth.
(In front): P.Warters, S.Flannery, L.Milner, P.Foster, C.Hunter.
(Insets): M.Sullivan, D.Goodwin and D.Sheehan.

(Right)
Vic Yorke the mighty goal kicking prop who was a rock of the York club into the 'sixties.

(Pictured, left)
York players training on the sands at Primrose Valley in 1961. Edgar Dawson passes to Bob Coglan, with Vic Yorke and Laurie Milner in close support.

* In 1963 York supplied two wingers for the Great Britain team in the Ashes series versus Australia - Geoff Smith and Mick Sullivan, the latter played the last of his record number of Tests as a York player.

(Above)
Willie Hargreaves the York full-back for over a decade.

Clarence Street packed as 12,259 crowd sees York in cup

A bumper crowd of 12,259 packed into Clarence Street to see York tackle Hull K.R. in the second round of the Challenge Cup in 1964. The Robins won 23-7 on their way to Wembley, after a titanic battle. York's points came from a try by the former inter-national winger Mick Sullivan, with two goals by prop Vic Yorke.
The York team was: Hargreaves; Smith, Hunter, Flannery, Sullivan; Sheehan, Evans; Yorke, Milner, Firth, Lamming, Goodwin and Elmer.
Pictured: **York forwards Dennis Goodwin and Vic Yorke join forces to get Hull K.R. prop John Bath into touch in that 1964 cup-tie.**

With the Amateurs

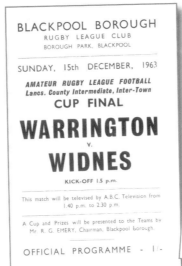

(Above) Action from the final qualifying round of the Challenge Cup in 1963, between York Imperial (light jerseys) and Moldgreen of Huddersfield (dark jerseys.) This game was, remarkably, played at Naughton Park, Widnes after many vain attempts to find a playable ground closer to home during the "big freeze" of that winter. Imperial won 8-nil and went on to lose 15-4 to Bramley in the first round proper.

As the programmes (above) illustrate, two of the most positive innovations in Amatur Rugby League during the 1960s were the live television coverage of junior games by A.B.C. Television, and the revival of an amateur league in London. With commentaries by the R.F.L. secretary Bill Fallowfield, the televised games left an indelible impression on fans across the north of England who got to see them. They were at their zenith during the 1963-64 and 1964-65 seasons, when Inter-town and County Championship games were covered, culminating in a memorable Under-19 international against France at Rochdale.

Other significant moves for the game outside the professional ranks came with the formation of the English Schools Rugby League and their first international in France in 1967; followed by the birth of the Universities Rugby League.

In the annual international matches with France, the England amateurs had a won four, lost five record at Open-Age level in the 'sixties. Among these ultimate corinthians of British sport, none was more outstanding than the Millom forward Ron Jackson, capped first as a junior international in 1961 and then a senior in 1964, 1967 and 1968 (as well as later in 1975 and '76). Of those amateur teams who reached the first round proper of the Challenge Cup, the closest to beating professional opposition were the Wakefield side Brookhouse, who entertained Doncaster at their own Barnsley Road playing fields in 1962, and went down by only 7-4 to the Dons (see programme above.)

1960s AMATEUR INTERNATIONALS

OPEN-AGE
1960 (Hull) - England 8, France 2.
1961 (Villefranche) - France 3, England 11.
1962 (St.Helens) - England 6, France 17.
1963 (Roanne) - France 16, England 15.
1964 (St.Helens) - England 5, France 8.
1965 (St.Gaudens) - France 10, England 18.
1966 (Warrington) - England 32, France 13.
1967 (Tonneins) - France 9, England 8.
1968 (Hull K.R.) - England 4, France 5.
1969 (La Reole) - France 2, England 2.
Totals: Played 10; France won 5, England won 4, one match drawn.

JUNIORS (Under-19)
1960 (Bordeaux) - France 21, England 13.
1961 (Wakefield) - England 2, France 15.
1962 (Limoux) - France 25, England 19.
1963 (Wakefield) - England 22, France 6.
1964 (Avignon) - France 13, England 9.
1965 (Rochdale) - England 14, France 12.
1966 (Avignon) - France 8, England 7.
1967 (Rochdale) - England 19, France 10.
1968 (Perpignan) - France 12, England 8.
1969 (Bradford) - England 7, France 15.
Totals: Played 10; France won 7, England won 3.

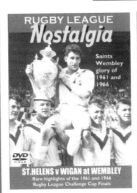

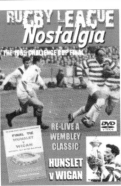
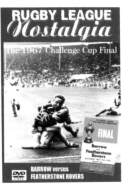
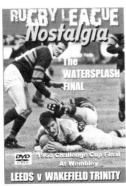

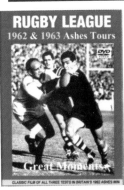

CUMBERLAND'S GAME

(Above) The Cumberland team before playing Yorkshire at Derwent Park in 1966. Left to right: *(Standing):* Louis Shepherd, Mr. Tom Stewart, Hedley Rodgers (masseur), Malcolm Moss, Dennis Martin, Mr. Tom Mitchell, Bill Holliday, Les Moore, Tony Colloby, Matt McLeod, Mr. Joe Tyson. *(In front):* Bob Wear, Harry Archer, Joe Southward, Paul Charlton, Brian Edgar (captain), Eddie Brenan, Billy Smith and Frank Foster.

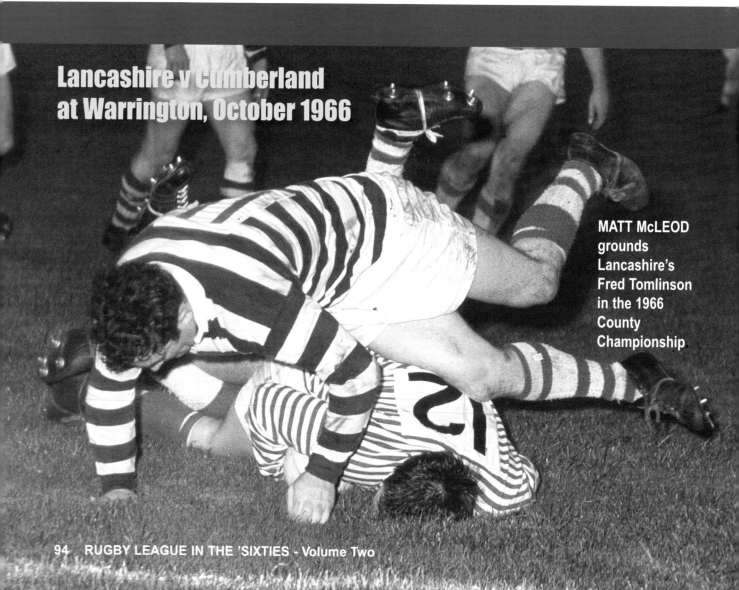

Lancashire v Cumberland at Warrington, October 1966

MATT McLEOD grounds Lancashire's Fred Tomlinson in the 1966 County Championship

After winning the County Championship four times in the first seven seasons of the 'sixties, Cumberland's crowning glory came in 1967 with their victory over a virtual Test strength Australian team. Their 17-15 win over the Kangaroos at Workington's Derwent Park ground is one that should have been celebrated far more in subsequent years than it has been - in the same way that Rugby Union has romanticised any of its provincial teams' victories over the New Zealand All Blacks - but Rugby League (and especially Cumberland) has grown used to seeing so many of its great moments in history being airbrushed away.

For Cumberland, just being granted a fixture against the Australians was a triumph in itself, as they had waited since 1948 to see the County side line up against the men in green and gold. The main insitigator behind getting the game was the Cumberland County Rugby League President, Tom Mitchell - and he was proud to begin his welcome to the Australians in the official programme by writing: *This fixture with our friend from down-under is the first of its kind for many a long year. For too long and for obscure reasons, the Tourist game in Cumberland has not been given full County status. Now with Cumberland County Champions during 1959, 1961, 1963, 1965 and 1966, this honour could no longer be denied them, and this was unanimously agreed by the International Committee of the Rugby League.*

Added delight for the Cumbrians was because, at last, they had a Saturday fixture against the tourists - Barrow's installation of floodlights meant they hosted the 1967 Kangaroos on the Thursday night during the tourists brief sojourn to the Lake District, hence Cumberland got to play against the "Saturday" team rather than the midweek boys. Famous names like: Langlands, Irvine, Billy Smith, Les Johns, Kelly, Sattler and Johnny Raper were in the Australian team which squared off against the Cumbrians in perfect conditions at Derwent Park on 18th November 1967.

Cumberland, wearing Workington Town colours of white with a blue band, led 17-7 before two late tries brought the Aussies back to a two point margin, both sides scored three tries (Cumberland's by winger Bob Wear (2) and the hooker Tom Hill) with the goal-kicking of their captain Bill Holliday making the winning difference. Holliday was an inspirational figure, and a reminder of the status of Cumbrians in the game in the 'sixties comes in the fact that he was also the Great Britain captain for all three Tests of that year's Ashes series; following on from another Cumbrian forward, Brian Edgar, who had led the Lions in the 1966 Ashes series.

The Cumberland team was: Paul Charlton (Workington); Bob Wear (Barrow), Ike Southward (Workington), Eric Bell (Workington), Keith Davies (Workington); Phil Kitchin (Workington), Sol Roper (Whitehaven); Bill Holliday (Hull K.R.), Tom Hill (Whitehaven), Dennis Martin (Workington), Bill Kirkbride (Workington), Les Moore (Whitehaven) and Bill Pattinson (Workington). *Unused substitutes:* Les Bettinson (Salford) and Matt McLeod (Whitehaven). The referee was Mr. J. P. Hebblethwaite of York.

The one disappointment on a wonderful day for Cumbrian Rugby League was that the attendance was below 10,000 - a crowd of 7,545 being recorded.

(Above)
Bill Holliday on Test duty for Great Britain in France in 1966, with full-back Ken Gowers in support. Holliday played magnificently to lead Cumberland to a famous victory over the Australians in November 1967.

(Above)
Bill Pattinson on the attack for Cumberland tries to evade Australian Graeme Langlands in the 1967 tour fixture.

Referees – men in the middle

(Below) Eric Clay pictured with the two French officials who acted as touch-judges, before refereeing the France versus Great Britain Test match in Paris in 1968. It was the third consecutive year Mr. Clay had taken charge of a Test match in France.

(Above) "The Sergeant Major" Eric Clay on the spot as Bill Sayer dives over to score for Wigan in the 1960 Championship Final at Odsal Stadium versus Wakefield. The beaten Trinity defenders are Derek Turner and Gerry Round, with Wigan's Brian McTigue up in support of Sayer.

Rugby League REFS!

The first team referees panel in the 1963-64 season

Grade One

C.F .Appleton (Warrington)	D.S. Brown (Dewsbury)
D.T.H. Davies (Manchester)	G. Davies (Wakefield)
R. Gelder (Wilmslow)	A.E. Durkin (Dewsbury)
J.Manley (Warrington)	L. Gant (Wakefield)
N.T. Railton (Wigan)	G. Philpott (Leeds)
R.L. Thomas (Oldham)	H. Pickersgill (Castleford)
E. Clay (Rothwell)	C. Whiteley (Ossett)
M. Coates (Pudsey)	G. Wilson (Dewsbury)
T.W. Watkinson (Manchester)	L. Wingfield (Normanton)
E. Lawrinson (Warrington)	F.J. Howker (Rochdale)
P. Geraghty (York)	J.P. Hebblethwaite (York)

Grade Two

H.G. Hunt (Culcheth)	R. Oliver (Wakefield)
S. Shepherd (Oldham)	G. Scott (Wakefield)
R. Welsby (Warrington)	H. Pearce (Leeds)
R. Appleyard (Leeds)	J. Senior (Bradford)
B. Hall (Wakefield)	B. Baker (Wigan)
H. Cook (Hull)	G.T. Schofield (Manchester)
T. Keane (Oldham)	H. Morgan (Oldham)

The 1960s was the decade when the cult of the "celebrity referee" was born in Rugby League, thanks largely to the growing influence of television and the BBC's commentator Eddie Waring. Always on the lookout for a personality, it was Eddie who dubbed Eric Clay "The Sergeant Major," and helped make him the game's most instantly recognisable referee.

Mr. Clay had served in the Royal Air Force in the war, and his military style discipline and no-nonsense precision, was perfect for the "Sergeant Major" tag. A large man physically, he had an intimidating presence in the eyes of many supporters and, certainly, players who broke the laws knew they would be off with a sharp blast of Clay's whistle. His status as the game's highest profile referee was confirmed when he won the accolade of controlling the first Wembley Cup Final of the decade, and this was the first to be attended by Her Majesty Queen Elizabeth.

(*Above*) **Young referee Fred Lindop makes his presence felt in his first Test match, pointing to the touchline as he sends off Australian forward Dennis Manteit for a high tackle on Roger Millward in the opening rubber of the 1967 Ashes series at Headingley. Cliff Watson, Tommy Bishop and Peter Flanagan look to get involved.**

Fred Lindop

As coincidence would have it, the second time the Queen was the Royal guest at the Rugby League Cup Final, in 1967, Eric Clay was again the referee. Another "first" for Mr. Clay came as he became the first man to referee a Great Britain Test match on overseas soil when he took the game against France in Perpignan in 1966. So impressed were the French that they invited Eric back to referee their Cup Final in 1967, the same year that George Philpott refereed the French Championship Final.

Among the other top referees of the time, several were school masters, notably: Joe Manley, Deryck Brown and D.T.H. (Dennis) Davies, who all brought an authority to their control of the game. And after the Australians had grown to fear "Sergeant Major" Clay on their 1963 tour, when they returned in 1967 they faced a brand new kid on the block in the shape of Fred Lindop. The Wakefield based whistler had a meteoric rise to the top of the refereeing ranks and he took charge of all three Tests in the 1967 Ashes series at the tender age of 27 - making Fred younger than several of the players he was in control of.

1960s WEMBLEY REFEREES
1960 - Eric Clay (Rothwell)
1961 - Tom Watkinson (Manchester)
1962 - Dennis Davies (Manchester)
1963 - Dennis Davies (Manchester)
1964 - Dickie Thomas (Oldham)
1965 - Joe Manley (Warrington)
1966 - Harry Hunt (Prestbury)
1967 - Eric Clay (Rothwell)
1968 - John Hebblethwaite (York)
1969 - Deryck Brown (Preston)

READ ALL ABOUT IT

Rugby League in the national newspapers

National newspapers played a very big part in Rugby League during the 'sixties, with almost every daily and Sunday paper having their own full-time correspondents, many of whom were promoted as high profile figures. With the national press producing their northern editions in Manchester, Deansgate was awash with big-name Rugby League writers.

But the biggest name of all, Eddie Waring, was one who was not based in Manchester as he maintained his base across the Pennines in the city of Leeds. Despite becoming best known as the BBC's t.v. commentator, Eddie maintained his newspaper role with the *"Sunday Pictorial"* which later marged into the *"Sunday Mirror."*

Their bitterest rival in the popular Sunday market was *"The People,"* whose Rugby League writer Phil King, a former county cricketer, was always in tough competition with Eddie Waring for the biggest scoops. With fixtures played on Saturdays, all the Sunday papers carried extensive match reports and pictures every week.

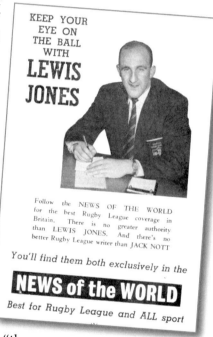

On weekdays, the popular papers brought a daily diet of Rugby League news fuelled largely by the quest for new signings and transfer deals, plus speculation over international selections and coverage of major tours and Test matches. High profile writers included: Jack Bentley *"Daily Express,"* Joe Humphreys *"Daily Mirror,"* and Allan Cave *"Daily Herald,"* the latter being recognised everywhere as "the man in the beret." The *"Daily Mail"* was one of the best newspapers for Rugby League in the 1960s, their number one correspondent was Derek Marshall, who later moved over to cover Rugby Union and was replaced by Brian Batty. The *"Daily Sketch"* had Neville Haddock as their full-time Rugby League writer whilst among the broadsheets, *"The Guardian"* had Harold Mather, one of Manchester's most respected and long-serving journalists, and the *"Daily Telegraph"* were well served by Bob Pemberton.

Although this was more prevalent in the major regional newspapers, some national papers also employed well known star players, or former players, to write columns - as this advert for Lewis Jones *(above)* writing for the *"News of the World"* illustrates. Most prolific of these was Joe Egan who wrote in the *"Sunday Express,"* whilst some of the big-selling Sundays were also known to produce controversial articles by stars like Alex Murphy and Mick Sullivan which ruffled a few feathers.

(Pictured)
Typical adverts from the 1960s promoting Rugby League's big-name writers - Phil King in *"The People"* and Jack Bentley in the *"Daily Express."* Phil King's scoops made his column essential Sunday morning reading for Rugby League fans, in the same way Eddie Waring had earlier dominated in the *"Sunday Pictorial."*

SATURDAY NIGHT SPECIAL

It was one of the great rituals of being a Rugby League fan in the 'sixties - following the match every Saturday afternoon, the evening couldn't come quick enough so you could get your hands on the *"Football Final"* newspaper.

Therein would be a blow-by-blow account of your local teams' games, plus all the results and up-to-the-minute league tables. In those pre-computer days of hot-metal printing, it was a remarkable feat of ingenuity to ensure that, within an hour of the final whistle being blown on those games, the *"Football Final"* papers would be out on the streets.

Copy for the reports was phoned in at regular intervals during the game by the local correspondent at the gound - if a telephone line was available in the press box - if not, it was ferried to the newspaper offices by copy-boys on bicycles. Action photographs would always be taken in the opening stages of the game, to allow time for the pictures to be developed and then the metal lithographic plates to be made ready to go to press. And every Saturday this operation would run like clockwork at top speed to ensure the papers were out on time, ready to be snapped up by eager Rugby League followers.

All areas had their own local *"Football Finals,"* and all had their own expert reporters who produced in-depth comment columns to go with the match reports. Those with the widest range included: the "Pink" produced by the *"Evening Post and Chronicle"* in Wigan; the "Green Post" produced by the *"Yorkshire Evening Post"* in Leeds; the "Yorkshire Sports" produced by the *"Telegraph and Argus"* in Bradford and the other "Pink" produced by the *"Manchester Evening News."*

In the northwest outpost of Whitehaven, despite not having a local evening newspaper actually produced in the town, Rugby League fans got no less than three different football papers covering their local team every Saturday (plus "A" team match reports.) It was a ritual to get all three - the first arrival, by 6 pm was the "Buff" from the *"Evening Star"* in Workington; next at 7 pm it was the "Green" from the *"North Western Evening Mail"* in Barrow (known by all simply as the "Barrow Mail;" and an hour later, by 8 pm, the *"Lancashire Evening Post"* would arrive hot foot from its presses in Preston.

Those Saturday night papers provided a great source of material for youngsters to start keeping scrapbooks, and were a very valuable way of practising literacy skills. In the 'sixties, before the advent of local radio stations covering Rugby League, and long before the invention of the internet, the *"Football Finals"* were the essential way of getting the latest news.

SCORE EVERY WEEK WITH THE GREEN!

Every week our team of reporters and photographers bring you the best detailed reports and action pictures of all the big games to keep you in touch with your favourite team So get the Green and be a winner yourself.

GREEN POST
Every Saturday

(Pictured)
At the top, a front page in 1966 from the "Football Pink" from the *"Post and Chronicle"* in Wigan. And below, Mick Shoebottom adorns an advert for the "Green" from the *"Evening Post"* in Leeds.

League's specialist magazines

A constant factor for Rugby League fans throughout he 1960s, just as it had been in the previous decade, was the presence of the game's very own weekly newspaper the *"Rugby Leaguer."* Every Friday throughout the season, from early August until the week after the Championship Final in May, the *"Leaguer"* would be devoured by supporters eager to keep up with news from all areas of the game.

With its bold motto of *"All for the good of the game,"* it was a newspaper which spoke with authority throughout the 'sixties, long before the word 'tabloid' entered the English language. Very knowledgable correspondents contributed weekly articles covering all the clubs, a mix of local newspaper reporters or the club secretaries, and among the most enjoyed columnists were Cyril Briggs and a young fellow who wrote under the name of Ramon Joyce - later to emerge as the highly respected *"Yorkshire Post"* correspondent Raymond Fletcher.

The *"Rugby Leaguer"* began the 'sixties being published by the Lockie Press company in Golborne, near Warrington; but in 1965 was taken over by South Lancashire

(Above)
The very first edition of A. N. Gaulton's *"Rugby League Magazine"* published in March 1963.

(Below)
Tom Webb's *"Rugby League Record"* issue number two, which appeared in October 1962, and featured the editor himself on the front cover in his role as schoolboy Rugby League coach.

Newspapers Limited and produced from their headquarters in College Street, St.Helens. The change of ownership saw a big increase in the photographic content, although the *"Leaguer"* initially continued to be printed on its distinctive green paper.

In addition to that weekly newspaper, many fans craved a monthly magazine to fill the gap left when *"Rugby League Gazette"* ended in 1958 after appearing in various different formats throughout the 'fifties. Tom Webb was the first man to take this particular plunge in the 'sixties when he launched his magazine *"Rugby League Record"* in September 1962. Tom, an Oldham schoolteacher and one of the game's greatest enthusiasts, was well known as a writer in the *"Rugby Leaguer"* with his *"Young Leaguers' Column"* sparking the enthusiasm of thousands of young supporters. Alas, *"Rugby League Record"* only lasted for three monthly issues before insufficient sales forced its closure.

Later the same season, in March 1963, another periodical saw light of day with the first edition of *"Rugby League Magazine"* published and edited by the Huddersfield based A. N. Gaulton. More modest in format, the pocket-sized *"Rugby League Magazine"* was published once every two months rather than monthly, and managed to survive throughout the rest of the 'sixties as a much enjoyed and respected source of record and historical reference. It only came to an end in 1970 with the sadly premature death of its publisher Norman Gaulton.